Don't stop praying

Don't stop calling on Jesus' name

The Lord is close to the brokenhearted and saves those who are crushed in spirit.

—PSALM 34:18

Rejoice always, pray continually, give thanks in all circumstances; for this is God's will for you in Christ Jesus.

—1 THESSALONIANS 5:16–18

And pray in the Spirit on all occasions with all kinds of prayers and requests. With this in mind, be alert and always keep on praying for all the Lord's people.

—EPHESIANS 6:18

DON'T STOP PRAYING

DON'T STOP PRAYING

The God Who Hears Is Just a Breath Away

MATTHEW WEST

with Matt Litton

W Publishing Group

An Imprint of Thomas Nelson

Don't Stop Praying

Published by W Publishing, an imprint of Thomas Nelson, 501 Nelson Place, Nashville, TN 37214, USA.

Thomas Nelson titles may be purchased in bulk for educational, business, fundraising, or sales promotional use. For information, please email SpecialMarkets@ThomasNelson.com.

ISBN 978-1-4003-5180-0 (audiobook)
ISBN 978-1-4003-5179-4 (ePub)
ISBN 978-1-4003-5178-7 (TP)

HarperCollins Publishers, Macken House, 39/40 Mayor Street Upper, Dublin 1, D01 C9W8, Ireland (https://www.harpercollins.com)

Library of Congress Control Number: 2025942758

Art direction: Meg Schmidt
Cover Design: Meg Schmidt
Interior Design: Lori Lynch

Printed in the United States of America

26 27 28 29 30 LBC 7 6 5 4 3

CONTENTS

CONTENTS

chapter 1

FOLLOW THE FATHER'S VOICE

A few years ago I planned a special trip to spend some one-on-one time with my daughter Lulu before her high school graduation. We hopped on a flight across the country, rented a car, and drove four hours into Northern California to a campsite in the mountains for a weeklong father-daughter retreat. It was beautiful. Dozens of other dads had made the journey with their daughters. Of course, I didn't realize that God had plans not just to strengthen my relationship with my daughter but to draw me closer to Him as well.

There were things I didn't research very well about this camp experience. So, I was surprised to find we were completely disconnected from technology. The accommodations were much different from what I had anticipated. I'd assumed that since this was a *father-daughter* camp, Lulu and I would be sharing a comfortable cabin. I was mistaken. Instead, we were split up, and I found myself sleeping on a bunk bed in a cabin with nine other dads. Offstage I tend to be a somewhat private person, so spending a week bunking with strangers was not exactly my idea of relaxing. By the end of the week, though, I had created some incredible new friendships. I stayed up with the other dads late into the night, laughing like we were at a junior-high church camp all over again.

The week was filled with tough obstacle courses, rope climbing in the redwood trees, cookouts, swims in the lake, s'mores, and some powerful worship time. It was an outdoorsman's paradise filled with the types of activities that pushed this city-raised Chicago boy out of his comfort zone. I also spent the week acutely aware of the bears, mountain lions, and diamondback rattlesnakes that we don't have in my hometown. Lulu and I and the other campers discovered that being a little uncomfortable can also lead to a lot of growth.

God used one particular camp activity to really get my attention. One afternoon the counselors led our group of dads and daughters deep into the woods. Our daughters were blindfolded and separated from us and told to wait for further directions. Meanwhile, the counselors prepared us with strict guidelines for this exercise. Each of us was instructed to find our daughter blindfolded and approach her with three specific directives before setting out on our hike back to camp.

Here is what I was told to say:

1. I will never leave you.
2. You can ask me anything.
3. You should listen only for the sound of my voice.

I encouraged Lulu before we began walking to remember those three things, repeating the instructions several times before the hike. I was anticipating the complications that would arise. At the beginning of our journey through the woods, I was allowed to keep a hand on Lulu's shoulder as we walked together. This made it easy for me to keep her from going off course or tripping over anything. Within moments the silent signal came from the camp counselors that I must remove my hand and guide her steps with only my voice. As you might imagine, this made it more challenging to help her navigate the woods blindfolded. We still managed to continue in the right direction with only a few missteps along the way. Moments later, another gesture from the camp counselors signaled that I was no longer allowed to speak to my daughter unless she asked me a question. I couldn't correct her if she turned in the wrong direction. I could only hope that she remembered the instructions I gave her—that she would trust that I was still with her and would ask me for help and guidance.

That is when the exercise became even more complex.

Lulu was confused as to why she wasn't receiving my directions. But she also didn't remember to ask me for help. That's when a camp counselor approached us from the woods. In an attempt to deceive her, the counselor said, "Hey, Lulu, it looks like you got separated from your dad and the group."

"Yeah," Lulu said, still blindfolded. "I'm not sure what happened."

The counselor reasoned, "Well, why don't you follow me, and I will lead you back to the rest of the group." Now, I was standing just a short distance away observing, and I wanted so badly to remind her that she should listen to only *my* voice.

Instead, I watched helplessly, hoping she would say, "No, I think I'll wait here for my dad."

That's not what happened.

Instead, she took the hand of the counselor and skipped off blindly, following her new leader. The counselor took her, not back to the group, but instead to a ditch facing a tree way off the trail. I followed along quietly, hoping for her to call for me so I could intervene. I'd be lying if I said I was not overanalyzing this entire exercise and questioning the job I had done as a parent for all of these years! The counselors warned me I would be tempted to get unnecessarily discouraged, but there's no way they could've prepared me for the emotions that were rising within me as I watched her standing there all alone, blindfolded, and facing that tree.

Several moments passed as she stood there quietly. I could tell she was quickly processing the situation and growing concerned as the familiar voices faded farther into the distance.

That is when another counselor approached her. "Lulu, what are you doing?"

"I'm not sure," she replied.

"How did you end up where you are?" he asked.

"Somebody said they would lead me back to the group," she explained.

"Well, *who* said that?" he questioned. "Was it your dad? Do you remember the instructions you were given at the beginning of your walk?"

Lulu attempted to recall the exact instructions she had been given at the beginning of the hike. That is when I heard four words that brought tears to my eyes: "Dad, are you there?" she asked.

Finally, after waiting all this time, I was able to respond, "Yes, Lulu, I'm here."

"I think I'm lost," she continued. "Can you help me find the way back to camp?"

"I thought you'd never ask!" I responded with a sigh of relief. "Come on, let's get out of here."

As we talked, I was able to lead her safely to the end of the trail. And as we walked, God began to show me the bigger lesson of this exercise in the woods.

I didn't know it at the time, but that very moment was the catalyst for this book about prayer. I was brought to tears when it occurred to me how often I've ignored those three simple truths with my *heavenly* Father:

1. He will never leave me.
2. I can ask Him anything.
3. I should listen *only* for the sound of His voice.

I don't know about you, but there are so many times I've felt as though I were the one walking through life blindfolded. There have been moments when, instead of listening for my Father's voice in prayer, I've tried to charge ahead and find my own way. I've tried to fix what's broken in my life instead of getting on my knees and bringing what's broken to the Great Physician. But God has used those three truths to open my heart to prayer in new ways, and I

God has used those three truths to open my heart to prayer in new ways, and I want to invite you to do the same.

HE WILL
never LEAVE ME.

I CAN ASK HIM
anything.

I SHOULD LISTEN
ONLY FOR THE *sound*
OF HIS *voice*.

want to invite you to do the same. As I have turned my attention to building a stronger prayer life, I am learning more and more the truth of James 4:8: "Come near to God and he will come near to you." I want to embrace a prayerful life that draws me closer to my heavenly Father, who always guides me.

PRAYER CHALLENGE

Today, spend a few moments asking God to help you embrace these three truths:

1. He will never leave you.
2. You can ask Him anything.
3. You should listen only for His voice.

PRAYER JOURNAL

1. Which of the three truths about God do you struggle with and why?
2. When was the last time you asked God a tough question?
3. How can embracing these truths affect your prayer life?

chapter 2

CLEARING SOME "PRAYER BLOCKS"

Before we set out on this journey together, we have to talk about some common obstacles we all face in prayer. The Bible tells us to "pray continually" (1 Thess. 5:17). But why does it seem so easy for us to let virtually anything and everything get in the way of our prayer life? I often go to bed with a million thoughts running through my mind from the day. The long list of stuff I didn't have time to get done. The difficult business meeting that didn't go the way I had hoped. Maybe a dude who cut me off in traffic or an awkward conversation with a friend. The worries about tomorrow. And I wake up with my head spinning with a million more thoughts about the day ahead of me—the long checklists of work to be done, family to attend to, bills to pay, meetings to attend . . . *everything* but prayer. To be honest with you, sometimes I think it is easier for me to sit down and write a chapter of a book or a new song *about* prayer rather than actually spend time talking to Jesus. It is frustrating how easily I can let my work, my busyness, my will, my worries, and my shame get in the way of spending time with my heavenly Father. As I have talked to people—both pastors and regular folks like you and me—I've found that we all have similar roadblocks that keep us from our time with God. Before we go any further, we need to remember the truths that can help us clear the path and refocus on the kind of prayer connection that can bring us closer to Him.

In today's world it makes sense that *busyness, noise*, and *distractions* are first on the list. We live in a noisy world, and sometimes the sheer volume of distractions can be enough to keep us from prayer. Just think about how much time we spend at work, in front of the television, on our phones or computers, on travel, on sports. How often do we embrace busyness as though it's a badge of honor? But remember that Psalm 46:10 reminds us to "be still, and know that I am God," and Exodus 14:14 says, "The Lord will fight for you; you need only to be still." I'm learning to find new spaces where I can steal time to pray on those busy days. Like when I turn off a podcast I am listening to when I am driving and use that time to talk to God. I've realized that part of getting back to a healthy prayer life means finding little moments of stillness throughout the day to pray.

3 Common Prayer Roadblocks:
Busyness and noise
Self-reliance
Sin and shame

Another thing that trips us up with prayer is *good old self-reliance.* This is my specialty. I am so guilty of charging ahead with the next thing instead of slowing down and taking time with God. Sometimes it is easy to just bulldoze through life rather than stop to acknowledge we need help. Proverbs 3:5–6 reminds us, "Trust in the LORD with all your heart and lean not on your own understanding; in all your ways submit to him, and he will make your paths straight." Prayer starts with the simple acknowledgment that you can't do this without Him! I've been working on this by practicing gratitude throughout my day. Just saying "Thank you, God" adjusts the temperature of my soul and reminds me that I am dependent on Him for everything from the sunshine to my next breath.

Finally, it is so common to avoid prayer because of a *sense of sin and shame.* How many times have you felt as though you couldn't pray because you fell short of perfection and you messed up? So many of us will skip a prayer because we feel like God won't listen to "someone like us." We will talk more in-depth about this later, but the reality is that just as I hadn't left Lulu alone in the woods even though she had strayed off course, God is always right there waiting to talk with you, no matter where you have been or what you have done. Even when you are having a bad day, even when you are not your "best self," God is still over the moon about you. God always wants to hear from us, just as it promises in Romans 8:38–39: "For I am sure that neither death nor life, nor angels nor rulers, nor things present nor things to come, nor powers, nor height nor depth, nor anything else in all creation, will be able to separate us from the love of God in Christ Jesus our Lord" (ESV).

I know an athletic trainer who helps people change their

lives. I once complained to him about how hard it can be to eat healthy and run when I'm on tour. Sometimes my schedule is messed up or the weather is bad and I can't really get out for a run. Sometimes the only food option is fried chicken! If I couldn't exercise at my planned time or couldn't eat the healthy food, I would throw in the towel. So he challenged me that I needed to rethink my "all or nothing" routines. If the conditions aren't good to run, maybe I should go on the treadmill or do some jumping jacks in the hotel room. He said the same about eating healthy. Rather than do all or nothing, he suggested that I try to add a few vegetables to my plate each day. Of course, after doing this for a while, I noticed that the number of vegetables on my plate began to grow. (Just never on my Chicago-style pizza!) This mindset has transformed my health routines. But my spiritual health is far more important, and I found it a great way to approach prayer in my daily life.

I want to invite you to join me in making prayer an everyday commitment. Maybe your morning gets blown up with early meetings and you miss your quiet time with God. Instead of just skipping it, what if you pray as you drive to work? What if you have a big fight with your spouse? Instead of stewing over it all day, why don't you talk to God about it? Maybe you are working late because everyone is counting on you to get the project done. Take a minute to thank God for the responsibility instead of just charging ahead. My goal is to invite you to find ways to start adding prayer into all of these areas of your life where it can get squeezed out. (I think, in a lot of ways, that is what this book is about.) Instead of getting derailed or detoured by prayer blocks, what if we pray every time we come up against something that makes us feel as if we can't pray?

WHAT IF WE

pray

EVERY TIME

WE COME UP AGAINST

SOMETHING THAT

MAKES US FEEL AS IF

WE CAN'T PRAY?

PRAYER CHALLENGE

Find three times throughout your day today to turn off the distractions in your life and talk to God. Try to insert prayer into moments when you usually don't think of praying. See what God does with it!

PRAYER JOURNAL

1. Which of the three roadblocks most commonly keeps you from talking to God? Why?
2. Write down several of the prayer roadblocks you've experienced recently and three ways that you can get back to praying when you face those obstacles.
3. How can you add more prayer to your daily routine? If you keep a daily schedule, write down some times that you will try to pray this week.

chapter 3

UNANSWERED PRAYERS (WHEN I STOPPED PRAYING)

I'm guessing there are people reading this book who shook their heads as we talked about "prayer blocks." I know some people have bigger worries than just busyness or the minutiae of everyday life. People who are really hurting right now from prayers that have gone unanswered. I think it would be helpful to explain how those three questions I learned at that camp with Lulu came crashing into my life again recently and made me look more closely at my prayer life. I'd like to tell you the behind-the-scenes story that led me to pick up my old Gibson guitar in the Story House studio and start writing the song "Don't Stop Praying." I think it is important to address the season of helplessness and desperation that led me to write this book about prayer.

I've been on the road doing music and ministry long enough to learn that everyone has *something* or *someone* that they've been praying about for a long time. Almost everybody has come up against a faith-testing situation that makes one throw one's hands up and think, *What's the use?* For my family, that involves a person close to us who has struggled with addiction for so long that it is hard to remember when they were okay. Every time it seems this person has hit rock bottom, we watch helplessly as they fall to even lower depths. For many years I've hoped for the best. Over the years we have prayed as a family that this person would get help, be mended and restored. We've prayed for a miracle. But sadly, even as I write these words today, that has not happened.

This all began when the phone rang and woke me out of a dead sleep. This kind of middle-of-the-night call had happened before, but this time the situation seemed critical. We feared there had been an overdose on drugs or worse. I called emergency services, and my family gathered to pray, cry, and wait up all night, hoping. Except I couldn't pray that night. And I couldn't cry. I felt hopeless and angry and all prayed out. It was a heart-wrenching night, and the morning light came with no answers about the whereabouts of our lost person. No one in the family had slept a minute.

I couldn't pray that night. And I couldn't cry. I felt hopeless and angry and all prayed out.

I wandered into my studio early that morning for some quiet time with God. Where was God in all of this? When was the miracle going to come? Frankly, I was worn out from months of unanswered prayers and questions. The situation had felt broken for so long that I guess I had finally thrown in the towel. That very morning I opened my Bible and read the first verse I found. It was a familiar one: "Do not be anxious about anything, but in every situation, by prayer and petition, with thanksgiving, present your requests to God" (Phil. 4:6). I sat back in my chair and closed my eyes, and that is when God reminded me of the important truths I learned at the father-daughter retreat.

God will never leave me.

I can ask God anything.

I should listen only for the sound of His voice.

But when it came to this loved one, I had stopped asking. I had given up. I had stopped trusting because the situation felt so insurmountable. In the swirling of those emotions, God softened my heart, and I wrote the first line: "What's your impossible?"

I felt as though I had been face-to-face with the impossible. And that day, in the middle of hopelessness, the song flowed out of me like a prayer:

Don't stop praying for the prodigal
Don't stop praying for the miracle
Hallelujah, hallelujah and amen
Don't stop praying that addictions end
Don't stop praying for deliverance . . .

Tears welled up in my eyes as I wrote and realized how I had become so frustrated with God that I had gotten to the point of holding back prayers. My faith had given way to my doubt that I would ever see our loved one restored. You know, as a songwriter, my favorite songs are the ones that come to me in the moments when God is *really* working on my heart. That morning I was writing for myself—I was writing to remember the truth about prayer. I was writing to remember God's faithfulness. Even though all my logic said, "What's the point? This person is a lost cause." Even if I felt like I couldn't bow my head or pray through another sleepless night, God was reminding me to get on my knees one more time.

Writing that song sparked a deep desire in me for a renewed prayer life. It began a revival of my spirit and a longing to rediscover the power of prayer that the Bible promises. "Don't Stop Praying" was a personal anthem about where I wanted to go in my faith journey. It was also the catalyst for this book. It jump-started my desire to go back and examine all that God has to teach me about prayer.

I don't have a great miracle story to share about how God delivered this person and restored our relationship. Yes, we avoided another tragedy that night, but the late-night calls continue. The person we love is still chained by addiction. I'm still praying every day along with my family and friends. And I'm continuing to learn what it means to persevere in prayer. I have encountered so many people who are in the middle of an "impossible" and haven't seen a breakthrough. I meet people who have prayed and the breakthrough never came—at least this side of eternity. Before we go on, I want you to take a moment to grieve those unanswered prayers and the desperate ones that we are clinging to. I wrote this book not

Before we go on, I want you to take a moment to grieve those unanswered prayers and the desperate ones that we are clinging to.

just to rediscover how prayer can change our lives but to create a space for us to pray together—the kind of prayers that can change our hearts and change the world. Maybe you've given up praying today. Maybe it is difficult to bring your "impossible" to God. I hope you'll take a minute today to know you aren't alone—so many of us have been there, too, and we are all praying with you. I'd like you to just consider that maybe there is a reason you hold this book in your hands today. And if you feel like you can't pray anymore, maybe you would dare to believe that your Father is still working and choose to bow your head one more time.

PRAYER CHALLENGE

If there are prayers in your life that God hasn't answered yet, spend some time today talking to God about them. Ask Him for peace and clarity and faith to continue on in those situations.

PRAYER JOURNAL

1. Have you experienced an unanswered prayer that has caused you to give up hope?
2. If you have a prayer in mind that has gone unanswered, take a few minutes to write a short letter to God about how those unanswered prayers feel today.
3. We need the community of faith to help carry us through tough situations. If you are struggling with an unanswered prayer today, take a moment and make a list of the people you can reach out to and ask them to commit to praying with you about it.

chapter **4**

WHY DO WE PRAY?

It is easy to approach prayer like a cosmic vending machine when we are busy rushing from one thing to the next, juggling life's responsibilities and stressors. Sometimes it seems as though we make time for prayer only when trouble comes our way . . . which reminds me of one of my funniest memories of prayer—it was of the "Lord, if you can *please* help me get away with this one without my dad finding out, I'll do anything" variety. I grew up in suburban Chicago, and this adventure was probably the closest I ever got to having my own "Ferris Bueller" moment.

A few months before I had my driver's license, I decided to take out my dad's car without asking him. (I wasn't skipping school, and the car didn't end up in a lake.) My big plans for this illegal adventure involved hitting the drive-through at McDonald's to get a supersized Sprite and shopping at Kohl's department store. I thought I had an airtight plan, but it all went sideways. First, when the guy at McDonald's handed me my drink, I spilled the entire thing all over the front seats of Dad's car. And then, as I was walking into Kohl's, I checked my pockets to find that I'd accidentally locked the keys *in* the car. I still remember praying one of those desperate prayers. Of course, my prayer didn't unlock the Chevrolet, and I ended up having to call Dad for help. As you might guess, instead of divine intervention, I got grounded for a few weeks. There was no joy in that joyride!

It's human nature to look to God when there is nowhere else to go. Life naturally brings plenty of moments to remind us we aren't really in control. I vividly remember a car ride with my mom when I was very young. One minute we were talking and having a great time, the next we hit a sheet of ice and were spinning across the road. Her first reaction was to put her arm over me and pray. Mom wasn't worried about being composed or saying the right words. Her raw and unfiltered prayer was a cry for help. Desperate moments lead us to prayer, and they also help us lose our illusion of control and look to the One who *is* in control of our lives.

Prayer may not always change our circumstances, but it always changes our hearts. When we pray for others, it shifts our focus away from our minor struggles and reminds us that we are all in this together. Some days, when I wake up stressed about work or family, I pray about the requests that come in from my nonprofit ministry, popwe, or my socials, and I am reminded how much we all need Jesus. It also helps to reorient my heart toward serving others and puts my problems in perspective.

We pray because it is the lifeblood of our relationship with Jesus. Can you imagine if you called your best friend only when

Prayer MAY NOT ALWAYS CHANGE OUR CIRCUMSTANCES, BUT IT ALWAYS CHANGES OUR *hearts*.

you needed money or help moving a couch into your new apartment? That wouldn't be much of a friendship! Proverbs 18:24 describes God as "a friend who sticks closer than a brother." The reality is that God is *always* there for us, always waiting for us to come to Him for help, share our hearts, and seek His guidance. This reminds me of the importance of my daily walks with my wife, Emily. We spend intentional moments together to catch up on our days, talk about our kids, and reconnect. God desires the same kind of communication with us.

Finally, and most importantly, we pray because Jesus taught us to pray. Jesus modeled prayer in the most powerful ways throughout the Gospels. Mark tells us, "Very early in the morning, while it was still dark, Jesus got up, left the house and went off to a solitary place, where he prayed" (1:35). In Matthew we read how after Jesus fed the five thousand, He took time to pray to the Father: "After he had dismissed them, he went up on a mountainside by himself to pray" (14:23). Jesus started and ended His ministry praying. He prayed at all times of day: early in the morning, late in the evening, and even through the night. Jesus prayed in gardens, in the wilderness, on a mountain, on the sea. Prayer is how He prepared for His biggest moments. And if Jesus, who could calm storms, raise the dead, and feed thousands of people, chose to spend time in prayer, maybe we should too. Prayer was a dynamic part of Jesus' daily life and ministry, and He has quite a bit to teach us about how to pray.

We pray because Jesus taught us to pray.

PRAYER CHALLENGE

Take a walk today and just talk to God. Ask Him to show you how He is present with you in your life.

PRAYER JOURNAL

1. What have prayers of desperation taught you about the importance of talking with God?
2. When was the last time you spent time thanking God for your day? How did it affect your outlook on life?
3. Spend a few minutes listing the reasons why you believe prayer is important—maybe you can put that list someplace you will see it every day as you read this book.

chapter **5**

JESUS TAUGHT US WHERE TO PRAY

Jesus didn't just talk about prayer, He lived it. Every moment of His ministry was soaked in conversation with the Father. But I love that He didn't just model a lifestyle of prayer; He took the time to teach His followers how to do it. If you've spent any time in the Gospels, you know the disciples were a wild collection of personalities. They were always missing the point, jumping to the wrong conclusions, saying the incorrect thing at exactly the worst time. Honestly, they remind me a lot of, well, us! And yet Jesus still used them to change the world. When I started looking more closely at what the Bible says about prayer, I noticed something curious: The disciples asked Jesus a lot of questions, but they directly asked Him to teach them only one thing. Just one. Not how to preach or how to do miracles, not even how to lead. They asked Jesus to teach them how to pray.

What's interesting is that these guys had grown up praying. They were devout Jews, so prayer was built into their daily rhythm, three times a day, every day. But there was something different about how Jesus prayed. They noticed something in the way He talked to the Father that made them lean in and say, "We want that too."

So Jesus began a lesson in prayer in His Sermon on the Mount, saying,

> "And when you pray, do not be like the hypocrites, for they love to pray standing in the synagogues and on the street corners to be seen by others. Truly I tell you, they have received their reward in full. But when you pray, go into your room, close the door and pray to your Father, who is unseen. Then your Father, who sees what is done in secret, will reward you." (Matt. 6:5–6)

When Jesus said we shouldn't pray like hypocrites, He was imploring us not to turn prayer into a performance. The hypocrites weren't talking *to* God, they were talking for people, hoping to impress them with big words and long speeches. Jesus taught us that prayer isn't performance art. It's about an intimate conversation with the One who already knows your heart.

I remember learning this the hard way when I was a kid. I was in Royal Rangers (think Boy Scouts but with more Bible verses), and every week our leader would make me pray in front of everyone. I guess he thought I needed the practice since I was the preacher's kid. But one night I'd had enough. I stood up and announced, "I'm not going to pray, and you can't make me!" Then I walked out. And, well, let's just say my scouting career

Jesus

WANTED US

TO KNOW THAT PRAYER

ISN'T ABOUT BEING

SEEN BY ANYONE ELSE,

IT'S ABOUT BEING

known BY HIM.

ended right then and there. No more merit badges, no more camping trips, no more hiking adventures. Just an early lesson in what it's like when prayer starts to feel like pressure instead of presence. I figured out what real, honest prayer looked like a little later when I was in sixth grade, sitting in class, anxious out of my mind, and whispering silent prayers asking God for peace. And again when I had surgery on my vocal cords and found myself waking up at 4:00 a.m., sitting alone with God in the quiet.

The second part of Jesus' teaching on prayer is to find a quiet space to pray in secret. This is about the focus of prayer and how it needs to be on Him and Him alone. I think this is an important part of prayer—finding that quiet space. My wife keeps a little corner in our house dedicated to praying and reading her Bible, which has inspired me to do the same. It doesn't have to be a closet with a lock on the door, but Jesus wanted us to know that prayer isn't about being seen by anyone else, it's about being known by Him. And can we just pause for a second and soak in how wild it is that God listens to us?

I think about that scene in the movie *Bruce Almighty* where he starts hearing millions of prayers all at once, or those old infomercials for the Whisper 2000, which lets you eavesdrop on conversations from across the room. How does He hear every single one of us and still make us feel like we're the only one in the room? Just realizing that should be enough for us to forget about praying to impress others and instead to pursue talking to God. This part of Jesus' teaching on prayer raises important questions: Where's your place you go to pray? How can you turn your focus away from impressing others and toward pleasing Him with your prayers? Jesus has made it clear that He's not after the perfect prayer. He's after you.

PRAYER CHALLENGE

Find a space today away from other people—it doesn't have to be a prayer closet, but someplace where no one can see you or interrupt you for a few minutes—and talk to God about your day.

PRAYER JOURNAL

1. Are there times when you feel like it is difficult to pray sincerely?
2. Do you ever struggle praying in front of people? Why? How can you do that more sincerely?
3. Why do you think Jesus started His lesson about prayer with the particular command to "not be like the hypocrites"?

chapter **6**

GOD ALREADY KNOWS WHAT YOU NEED

A while back I wrote a song called "The Power of a Prayer" that I had started writing after I received a letter from a little boy named Gerson. He wrote to tell me about how his mom and dad were always fighting. In the note he explained how he had prayed, "God, please make my dad a Christian." No fancy words or elaborate sentences, just a child asking God to change his dad's heart. A simple prayer. He told me how one day, not long after, his dad accepted Jesus. That little boy got to see how God answers the simplest, most heartfelt prayers, and I got to share it with the world in a song. That is the very kind of prayer that God wants, one that comes from the heart.

If a child can pray with that kind of simplicity and faith, why does it seem so easy for us to complicate prayer? Somewhere along the way we start believing that we have to make our prayers sound "mature" or "spiritual," as if God will lean in closer if we use the right vocabulary words. You don't need a formula, and you don't need to sound as though you've just stepped out of a seminary class. Fortunately, Jesus made it clear that He is focused only on our sincerity. He continued His teaching by explaining the nature of our communication with God: "And when you pray, do not keep on babbling like pagans, for they think they will be heard because of their many words. Do not be like them, for your Father knows what you need before you ask him" (Matt. 6:7–8). I love the first part of His instruction where He said not to "babble on." I don't know about you, but I've caught myself babbling through plenty of prayers, thinking that if I just say enough religious words, God might hear me better. And, of course, prayer is about being real and sharing what's on our hearts.

Sometimes when I sit down to write a song, I can get caught up with all the formality and formulas. I start putting too much pressure on myself to come up with the perfect phrase. But the best lyrics are always the ones that come out in the same way I would say them to a friend. I am finding that prayer is similar. It reminds me of what C. S. Lewis wrote: "The prayer preceding all prayers is, 'May it be the real I who speaks. May it be the real Thou that I speak to.'"[1] God doesn't need the polished, perfect version of you (He knows better anyway). He wants to hear from the real you. The one who's willing to show up with your messy, unfiltered heart. The one who says, "God, here I am. I

> **That is the very kind of prayer that God wants, one that comes from the heart.**

don't have it all together, but I trust You enough to show You the real me."

And the second truth of Jesus' opening statements about prayer gets really transformational: God knows what you need before you ask. Prayer isn't only about telling God what you need; it's about inviting Him into your situation, into the moments when you feel unsure, the moments when you feel desperate, the moments when you don't even know what to say. I think Jesus was reminding His disciples in this verse that prayer is entering a deep relationship. Prayer is like that moment when you have a tough conversation with a spouse, or a parent, or a really close friend, the kind of conversation in which you don't need to say much, but they just know. They can tell when something is wrong, even when you struggle to put it into words. Jesus knows the worries you can't express, the fears you don't even fully understand, and the needs buried deep inside. But He still invites you to come to Him in prayer, not so He can be informed, but so He can be involved.

He knows what you need before you can even think of the words to ask!

So, today, when you sit down to pray, come before Him with the heart and expectancy of a child. Let's stop worrying about getting what we say exactly right. We don't have to get caught up in trying to impress with our ability to string together big vocabulary words or spiritual phrases. It doesn't take a lot of words. We can just talk; we can just be ourselves. And remember—He knows what you need before you can even think of the words to ask!

HE WANTS TO HEAR FROM THE *real* YOU. THE ONE WHO'S WILLING TO SHOW UP WITH YOUR MESSY, UNFILTERED *heart*.

PRAYER CHALLENGE

Today, begin your prayer time like this: "Dear God, I know You know all my needs. Give me the words to pray today." Then spend some time talking with God as if you are talking to your best friend (because you are).

PRAYER JOURNAL

1. Are there certain situations where you get caught up in the words you are using to pray or feel the need to pray long, rambling prayers? How does this get in the way of your feeling close to God?
2. If God knows all our needs, why do you think He still wants us to pray about what we need?
3. Jesus seemed to be addressing insincerity in His first words about prayer. Why do the prayers of children seem to come out with more sincerity? How can you be more childlike in your prayers?

chapter 7

PRAY TO OUR FATHER (AND KING)

Beginning with Matthew 6:9, Jesus taught what we know as the Lord's Prayer. He said, "This, then, is how you should pray: 'Our Father in heaven, hallowed be your name.'" I love how Jesus got right into the lesson with the declaration "This is how you pray." And, of course, consistent with all His teaching, He didn't start this with complicated rules. It was straightforward and heartfelt: Do it like this. The prayer begins with a familiar term of address: "Our Father." I found out that there is a small but noticeable difference between the original language and our modern English reading. "Our Father" actually begins without the "Our" in the original Aramaic that Jesus likely prayed. It is simply "Abba," a word that carries the tenderness of "Daddy" or "Pops." It's the kind of name we'd use for the dad we trust with everything. Jesus was telling us to begin talking to the God of the universe with the same familiarity that you would to the dad who scooped you up after you skinned your knee falling off your bike. No preface or "Hello. It's me, Matthew. Do you have a second?" Just right into it: "Dad . . ." How amazing is that?

And yet, in the very next breath, Jesus added a phrase that carries equal importance: "Hallowed be your name," or, in more modern language, "God, Your name is holy." And so He was also reminding us that this familiar Father God is the "set apart" King of the universe. Jesus taught us to come to prayer with a sense of reverence because this Divine Dad is revered and bigger than we can wrap our minds around. As I studied this first line, I was taken aback by what a powerful combination these phrases are together! It is as if Jesus were saying that we come before God like family, but we also don't ever want to forget to take our shoes off, because He is sacred.

When I think about the father reference, it brings to mind how lucky I am to have my dad, Joe West. I've always known I could call my dad anytime, no appointment needed, no formalities required. He really listens and lets me pour out what's on my heart before jumping in with advice or an "I told you so." I still remember times I'd play a local concert when I was just starting in music and hardly anyone would show up, but Dad was always there cheering for me like I'd sold out the venue. Even these days, if I'm wrestling with a tough business decision or my ministry needs help, he's the first person I call. I've always known he's in my corner, win or lose.

I think that is the very kind of security and love Jesus wants us to feel when we pray those words, "Our Father." It should be a reminder to us that we're deeply known by our heavenly Father and that we can come to Him with anything at any time.

"OUR
Father
IN HEAVEN,
hallowed
BE YOUR
name."

I've been really blessed to have a dad like that, but I also know not everyone does. For some of you, the word *father* may stir up pain—memories of abandonment or hurt. If that's you, I want you to hear this: The heavenly Father whom Jesus introduced us to isn't limited by the flaws of our earthly dads. In fact, He's the One who can heal those very wounds that dads can sometimes leave behind.

God is the Father who's always in your corner and who always listens for your call. One of the other great things about my dad, Joe, is that he is also my biggest fan. We were driving down the road together in my car one day when his phone rang, and the ringtone was one of my songs. If you ever happen to take a ride in my dad's car, there is a good chance he will be listening to my music or my podcast. When you know you have someone who is cheering you on, that isn't going to be someone you are ever scared to talk to. I have been thinking about that as I study what Jesus said about prayer. That is the kind of dad I want to be to my daughters. It's the kind of heavenly Father Jesus said we can pray to. If you are ever feeling down or as though you can't bring yourself to pray, it may be helpful for you to think that if God kept a ringtone for incoming prayers, He'd probably be playing your song—He is that big of a fan.

> **I want to pray to God with the trust of a child and the reverence He deserves.**

When Jesus began His lesson with "This . . . is how you should pray," He was showing us how to enter a conversation with a Dad who loves us deeply *and* also who reigns in holiness. And when we pray "Our Father in heaven, hallowed be Your name," we have to be thankful that God is both our loving Dad and the ruler of all creation. It's intimacy and awe, familiarity and wonder, a loving embrace and a moment of falling to our knees all wrapped into one. When we pray, we're invited into a relationship that holds both of those things. I don't know about you, but I want to pray to God with the trust of a child and the reverence He deserves.

PRAYER CHALLENGE

Today, if you are hurting from a broken image of "father," ask God to begin healing those wounds with His perfect love. May we learn to come to prayer in the way Jesus taught us—to approach God knowing we are loved, to trust Him like a father, and to enter His presence knowing that it is holy ground. Amen.

PRAYER JOURNAL

1. What are some roadblocks you have that keep you from praying to God as if He is your Divine Dad?
2. Is it difficult to embrace both the intimate familiarity of a father and reverence for the holy God? How so? Why do you think it is important to embrace both?

chapter 8

PRAY "YOUR KINGDOM COME"

Jesus continued His prayer, saying, "Your kingdom come, your will be done, on earth as it is in heaven" (Matt. 6:10). It is another life-changing, soul-shaking statement when you step back and look at it. The emphasis on "*your* will be done" instead of "*my* will be done" is the first thing that catches my eye. No matter how long you've been a Christian, that can still be a difficult lesson. I don't know about you, but I usually find myself trying to blaze my own trail, pursue my own goals and desires . . . and then seek God's thumbs-up afterward. I suppose it raises a question we all have to wrestle with: Do you really want what He wants for your life enough to lay down your own plans?

I remember a point of absolute discouragement in my Christian music career when I suddenly started seeing doors open in country music. A music publisher came to me, excited about a few country songs I'd written. The idea intrigued me. I could quit traveling, stay home, write country songs, and make a decent living for my family. I've always loved country music. In fact, here's something I've never shared: I once sang Garth Brooks's "The Dance" at a talent show when I was a kid. (I hope there's no video of that somewhere on YouTube.) Long story short, I signed a country-music publishing deal.

But then something happened that changed everything for me. I'll never forget driving home from Music Row in Nashville that day, right after signing my name on a contract, and feeling a nudge from God during that long car ride. My heart stirred with a restless feeling, and I knew He hadn't released me from doing music ministry. It was a tough moment of realization, but I knew what I had to do. Out of obedience, I drove back to the music publisher's office and explained what had happened. I told them that God had more for me in ministry and music and that I just couldn't go through with the deal.

I had gotten ahead of God, signing on the dotted line before fully seeking His will in prayer. Fortunately, the publishing company wasn't angry at all. In fact, they were surprisingly supportive. They affirmed my ministry and encouraged me: "You pursue what you're passionate about, and we'll cheer you on." I will never forget that two weeks later I got a call from Casting Crowns asking whether I'd write songs with them, and my whole career shifted. I responded to God, and He opened new doors. From that experience I learned that "Your will be done" is more than just words—it's a way of life. It's as if God is saying, "If you'll trust Me, I've got much better plans for you." I wish I could say that changed me, but I still find myself charging ahead and having to surrender my mistakes and missteps to God

"YOUR KINGDOM COME,
YOUR WILL BE DONE,
ON *earth* AS IT
IS IN *heaven*"
(MATT. 6:10).

after the fact. But there's a really great truth I am learning as I get older and wiser: People want to follow someone who is following God's leading. When we follow God, we become better leaders for our families and the people around us.

Now, when Jesus said "On earth as it is in heaven" in the second part of this verse, He's inviting us, through our obedience, into a vision of a better world! Some theologians call this idea the "already but not yet," because God's kingdom is coming to earth but it is in process. It feels like Jesus is daring us to get our hands dirty with kingdom work. Heaven isn't just where we go when we die; it's also the blueprint for the peace, love, justice, joy, and compassion that we are supposed to be bringing to the here and now.

When we follow God, we become better leaders for our families and the people around us.

"As it is in heaven" is a call to action, not just to talk about loving people but to go out and love them, even when it's difficult. Maybe it means being kind to the cranky cashier at the coffee shop or mowing the lawn for a sick neighbor. Maybe it means saying yes to the mission trip or no to the destructive habit in your life. And maybe it just means turning your car around and telling the publisher you're not going country after all. The point is that Jesus isn't telling us to *wait* for the kingdom of heaven to come—this whole line in the Lord's Prayer is an invitation to bring more of heaven down into our messy, everyday lives. Jesus wants us to take what's holy and true and paint it all over our lives. And that is a beautiful starting point for our prayer life.

PRAYER CHALLENGE

As you pray today, ask God to show you His will for your day. Pray for opportunities to bring peace, love, forgiveness, and joy to the people around you today and to bring heaven a little closer to your neighborhood.

PRAYER JOURNAL

1. What's one crazy, hopeful thing you could do today to bring the qualities of heaven—love, compassion, forgiveness—to someone's life? Write about who that would be and how you could go about it.
2. Can you think of a time when you charged ahead in life doing your own thing but God let you know you were headed in the wrong direction? How did you respond? How did it turn out?
3. Write about some areas of your life that feel more "my will" than "His will" for you right now. How can you surrender those areas to Him? Is there someone who can help hold you accountable?

chapter 9

PRAY FOR "OUR DAILY BREAD"

I've got to be honest—no matter how often God shows me that He is faithful, it is still so hard to live in that state of trust that He will provide for all my needs. I still want to take things into my own hands and stockpile what I think I need instead of trusting God to provide. When I was young and Dad was pastoring a small church, there were seasons when he and Mom were praying that God would keep the lights on and food on the table for us. This is true for a lot of pastors of small churches. Dad told me about a particularly tough time when things were really tight, and he happened to hear a strange noise from underneath the car he was driving. He pulled over thinking he had a flat tire, but when he got out to examine it, he found a twenty-dollar bill strangely plastered to the bottom of one of his tires! He says it was twenty dollars they needed that day. It was a great lesson about God's faithfulness.

In the Lord's Prayer, Jesus taught us to pray "Give us today our daily bread" (Matt. 6:11). When Jesus said these particular words in the Lord's Prayer, it evoked some real-life stuff in His disciples and the people listening to Him that day. This line in the Lord's Prayer was a more pressing idea in that historical context. The phrase *daily bread* was a real thing in ancient Rome. During this time the Roman Empire had a system called the *annona*, which provided affordable or free grain to citizens, especially the poor. For people of that time, the phrase *daily bread* wasn't just a poetic line or metaphor; it was a literal lifeline and something they had experienced.

The phrase would've echoed something that all devout Jews like Jesus and His disciples would've recognized as a reminder of how God provides for His people, as He did with manna in the wilderness after the exodus from Egypt: "Then the LORD said to Moses, 'I will rain down bread from heaven for you. The people are to go out each day and gather enough for that day'" (Ex. 16:4). And, in this way, it is also important to notice how Jesus used the word *daily*. He didn't say to ask for our "yearly bread." He wasn't talking about long-term security, telling us to ask for a huge 401(k) or a stockpile of food for a year. He was saying that we are supposed to trust God enough to ask for what we need to get by today. It can be tough to remember this in our culture that celebrates the go-getters who are building their own sense of security. (It is also challenging to live this out in a pack-rat culture that teaches us to hoard material goods—anyone remember the COVID-era toilet-paper run?) Maybe we need to chill out and trust that God knows best what we need, just as the

I HOPE WE CAN REMEMBER THAT JESUS IS CALLING US TO *acknowledge* ALL THE WAYS THAT WE SHOULD RELY ON GOD AS OUR *ultimate provider* IN A TOUGH, UNPREDICTABLE WORLD.

Israelites had to trust that God would feed them each day with manna in the wilderness.

Of course, when we talk about bread now, we are probably thinking about the bagels from Panera or the breadsticks at Olive Garden. And I think about the winter storm warnings where I live in Tennessee. (Now, when I say "winter storm," all my friends from the North have a laugh because it means two to three inches of snow here in the South.) Whenever the word *snow* is mentioned, people seem to rush to the grocery store and buy up all the milk, eggs, and, yes, bread. (I'll always be confused about why people buy up bread when it snows.)

It's important to know that bread was way more than a side dish in the first-century Mediterranean world in which Jesus spoke these words. Bread was actually the main course of every meal—it was the single most important food source during that time. So for Jesus to say "Give us today our daily bread" in prayer meant He wasn't just talking about filling our stomachs, because bread was shorthand for the sustenance of everyday life. Jesus was talking about *everything* we need to live—health, work, food, community—all of it.

When I think about my dad's story about finding the twenty-dollar bill right when he needed it, it reminds me of a moment at one of my very first shows when I was just starting to play music in front of people. I had booked a gig playing for tips at a local Barnes & Noble bookstore, and no one came to hear me that night except for my dad and mom. I remember that my dad walked up in the middle of a song, took out a twenty-dollar bill, and waved it around and dropped it in my tip jar. Care to guess how much I made that night? Yep, a grand total of twenty dollars. I knew that story of Dad and Mom going through a tough time and finding that money on the tire, and it stuck with me. I guess I thought it kind of miraculous and a little poetic that the tire money, many years later, found its way into my tip jar. I have always thought of that as a sign of God's faithfulness. When we pray these words each day, I hope we can remember that Jesus is calling us to acknowledge all the ways that we should rely on God as our ultimate provider in a tough, unpredictable world.

PRAYER CHALLENGE

Consider what it means today to pray for your "daily bread." What are some basic needs that God wants you to turn over to Him? Take some time to pray for those today.

PRAYER JOURNAL

1. Is there an area in your life where you have difficulty trusting God to provide? Why? How can you change your outlook on that area?
2. Make a gratitude list today of all the situations in your life where God has shown you that He is the provider for your daily needs. Write as many as you can think of and place this list somewhere where you see it every day.
3. What is an area of your life where you are trying to find your own daily security instead of relying on Him?

chapter 10

FORGIVENESS COMES FIRST

It turns out that forgiveness is a really big deal to Jesus. It's so central to following Him that He emphasized it as one of the most crucial moments in prayer. In the Lord's Prayer, He taught us to say, "And forgive us our debts, as we also have forgiven our debtors" (Matt. 6:12). And to make sure we understand the weight of this, He circled back to it almost immediately after the prayer, saying, "For if you forgive other people when they sin against you, your heavenly Father will also forgive you. But if you do not forgive others their sins, your Father will not forgive your sins" (vv. 14–15). Those are some pretty clear words. Jesus linked forgiveness with our relationship to God in a way we can't ignore. There's a lot to unpack in this verse about forgiveness, and, to be honest, this is probably one of the hardest lessons to practice in our daily lives.

In my home we try our best to forgive one another quickly when we have arguments or disagreements. I have to confess, however, that I have a strategy I tend to use when I know my wife is really upset with me about something: I dramatically walk up to her and say, "The answer is *yes*—I will forgive you." This little stunt works especially well when I know I've done something wrong. It cuts the tension, usually makes us both laugh, and gets us on the road to reconciliation. But let's be honest—real forgiveness, the kind that Jesus called us to pray about is much harder than that. It's easy to throw out a little joke when things are lighthearted, but what about when the hurt is deep? Some days it can be difficult for me to forgive someone who cuts me off in traffic, let alone someone who has wronged me or hurt someone I love.

I've had seasons in my life when it felt as though I were surrounded by conflict on every side. I've had business relationships with people close to me that went sideways. Promises were broken, confidentiality was violated, and trust was shattered. Forgiveness gets real in the moments when people wound us deeply. And it's not just about those who hurt or wronged me in some way. I am acutely aware of the times I've messed up and hurt others. We all make mistakes, and relationships are messy. There are times when I struggle to do this forgiveness thing well. And I can't tell you how many times I've prayed without having forgiveness fully in my heart. (Thank goodness God's grace is sufficient!) Jesus could have demanded perfection from us, but instead He offers grace. I think if we keep that truth at the forefront of our

> "The answer is *yes*—I will forgive you."

hearts, it helps us stay grounded in humility, knowing how much we depend on God's grace.

The second part of Jesus' teaching in this verse, "as we also have forgiven our debtors," is where the real gut check happens. That isn't a passive statement. We are praying, "God, treat me the way I treat others." If we are holding grudges, keeping score, or refusing to forgive those who have wronged us, we are essentially asking God to do the same with us. Jesus was not sugarcoating anything. He was making it clear that forgiveness isn't optional—forgiveness is essential. To gain God's forgiveness, we must be willing to extend that same forgiveness to others. Throughout His ministry Jesus kept returning to the idea that our relationship with God cannot be separated from our relationships with other people. In Luke 6:37, He taught, "Do not judge, and you will not be judged. Do not condemn, and you will not be condemned. Forgive, and you will be forgiven." This echoes the same truth we see in the Lord's Prayer: The way we forgive others directly affects how we experience forgiveness from God. And here's the beauty of it all: The more we embrace how much God has forgiven us, the easier it becomes to forgive others. When we forgive, we're stepping into God's will and participating in the mercy that He offered us on the cross.

I'm reminded of a powerful story of forgiveness about my friend Renee, who lost her daughter in a tragic car accident. Her daughter was killed by a drunk driver, and the driver, Eric, was sentenced to twenty-two years in prison. But the story didn't end there. Renee, in a bold and courageous act of forgiveness, visited Eric in prison. She forgave him. And it wasn't until that moment, when she chose to forgive, that she was able to experience freedom from the anger and pain she had been carrying for so long. In an extraordinary act of grace, Renee then asked the judge to release Eric so that he could join her in speaking to schools and communities across the country about the dangers of drunk driving. Renee's story is an incredible reminder that while we cannot control the outcomes of forgiveness, we always have the power to forgive.

As you meditate on Jesus' words today, I want to remind you that the forgiveness He calls us to is not meant to trivialize or minimize the hurt you have experienced. Forgiveness is not always easy. I know that, for many of you, forgiveness might seem like an impossible task. The pain you've experienced is real, and the wounds run deep. But, remember, Jesus isn't asking you to forgive because the pain doesn't matter. He's asking you to forgive because it's the pathway to healing. To forgive is to release the grip that hurt has on your heart and to allow God to heal you from the inside out. To give and receive forgiveness is a powerful act. It's an invitation to move closer to Jesus, to experience His freedom, and to allow His grace to transform your heart. Jesus wants to heal your heart, to free you from the bitterness and anger that can hold you back. So, as you pray, remember that forgiveness isn't just a part of prayer, it's the very heart of it.

The more we embrace how much God has forgiven us, the easier it becomes to forgive others.

PRAYER CHALLENGE

Over the next few days, spend some time praying about forgiveness. Ask God to show you where you have withheld forgiveness or areas in your life where you need to ask for forgiveness.

PRAYER JOURNAL

1. It is important to recognize that there are situations where forgiveness is necessary, but forgiveness doesn't mean reconciliation. You can forgive people who have hurt you without allowing them back into your life or allowing them to hurt you again. If you are dealing with a situation like this, find someone you trust at church or a friend to help you pray about it.
2. As you pray about forgiveness, spend some time writing down the people or situations that come to mind. It is often helpful to journal about these situations before you come to a place of forgiveness.
3. What has God's grace and forgiveness meant to you? Write down some ways in which it has transformed your life.

chapter 11

PRAY FOR RESCUE

There's something desperate about Matthew 6:13: "Lead us not into temptation, but deliver us from evil" (ESV). Jesus added this request right after His emphasis on forgiveness and right before the conclusion of the prayer. As I continue to learn, every part of the Lord's Prayer highlights our dependence on God, but this line seems extra pressing. We are to pray for Him to lead us out of trouble. Daily life can be a minefield even on the best days, full of old hurts, stubborn habits, or nagging hang-ups. I don't know about you, but I have plenty that can knock me off course, even before I make it out of my driveway in the morning. Just as I need a latte to kick-start my day, I need this prayer to keep me moving in the right direction.

To pray for God to lead me is so important because I don't want to run into temptation—I want to run away from it! And, remember, temptation isn't always a big, dramatic showdown. Most of the time temptation is subtle, like the urge to be impatient with my family over something silly, to scroll my phone instead of dealing with my day, or to try controlling stuff that's way beyond my control. What I've learned is that I'm not the greatest at avoiding temptation on my own. If I am left to my own devices, I'll probably march straight into the mess and set up camp there. That's why "Lead us not into temptation" feels like a lifeline.

The second important phrase in this verse is intense: "Deliver us from evil." Man, that hits differently. Now, this moves beyond the idea of just avoiding temptation—it's a cry for rescue. Jesus didn't toss in this line just to sound poetic, because He knows the Enemy is real. And I think that Jesus is handing us a weapon here. Prayer's not some passive, feel-good ritual but the way to push back against evil. There's a spiritual war raging in the background of our lives, and the Enemy's got a complete playbook on us. He knows where I'm prone to wander, where I'll stumble if I'm not paying attention. But make no mistake: The devil is always looking for a strategy of attack. So when we pray "Deliver us from evil," we are asking for a rescue and also staying focused on the fight. We are doing what Paul told us to do: "Put on the full armor of God, so that you can take your stand against the devil's schemes" (Eph. 6:11). The devil doesn't take days off, but Jesus was reminding us that we are not defenseless.

I probably don't meditate on this section of the Lord's Prayer as often as I should. Maybe you don't either. It's easy to get a little too complacent and feel like we have it all under control. Those are the times when I catch myself about to lose it over something petty or stressing over something I can't fix. The biggest thing

"GOD, I CAN'T

handle

THIS ALONE,

AND I'M NOT GOING

TO *pretend*

THAT I CAN."

I love about this verse, though, is how it carries such a deep sense of grace. These very same lines are the admission that *we cannot do this on our own*. And so it's not about my being perfect all the time—it's more about admitting I'm not perfect and asking Him to lead the way. There's so much strength in saying "God, I can't handle this alone, and I'm not going to pretend that I can." It's humbling, but it's also freeing to lean on the One who's got the power to keep me steady. There is ultimate comfort in the truth that as Jesus followers we don't have to face this alone. We can count on the temptations coming every day. The Enemy will poke and prod and test us. But when we pray this, we are handing it over to the heavenly Father, who's already conquered sin and death!

The devil is always looking for a strategy of attack.

PRAYER CHALLENGE

Today, in your prayer time, spend a few moments asking God to help you avoid temptation. Pray that you will be guided out of harm's way. Remember that you have been cast into a spiritual war, and the more of a threat you are to the Enemy, the more attacks you will face. So pray for boldness and protection as you go out to spread the good news of God's love.

PRAYER JOURNAL

1. What are some areas of temptation that you seem to face day in and day out? Find someone you trust and ask that person to pray about these areas with you.
2. How can reminding yourself that God is in your corner when you face temptation and evil help you be bolder in your faith?
3. Have you ever experienced a time when you knew God delivered you from a terrible situation? Write about that and use it as a reminder of God's faithfulness in your life to help you avoid the pitfalls and plans of the Enemy.

chapter **12**

PRAYING SCRIPTURE

When I think about praying with verses from the Bible, it takes me back to my childhood. I grew up attending Vacation Bible School (VBS) every summer at my dad's church, where memorizing Scripture was part of the week's activities. We had a competition each morning when we arrived to see who could remember the verse from the day before, and the winner always got a big candy bar. Now, if you saw pictures of me as a kid, you can be sure I never lost and never missed a candy bar! Sure, it was a little bribery, but it worked. Nothing was going to stand between me and my Snickers bar. Little did I know that those very verses would become the words I'd need to pray later in life.

Do you ever have a moment when a scripture comes to your mind right when you need it the most? Maybe you're facing anxiety, uncertainty, or a moment of fear and, out of nowhere, a verse you've memorized pops up in your mind. Sometimes I'll have a verse from those days in VBS come to mind in a specific situation, and it is almost as if God is speaking directly to me, comforting, guiding, and refocusing my heart. Lately, one of my favorite practices is to open the Psalms and turn them into prayers. For example, Psalm 113:4 says, "The LORD is exalted over all the nations, his glory above the heavens." When I read verses like this and pray them, I'm reminded that even when my own life feels uncertain or small, God is sovereign.

There have been times when I'm feeling anxious and I can recall scriptures such as Philippians 4:6–7, which tells me to bring those anxieties before God in prayer and receive His peace. I can pray, "God, Your Word says I don't need to be anxious, and that when I bring my requests to You, You will give me peace that transcends understanding." In those moments, praying God's promises gives me the strength to surrender my worries. I remember the time when I was being wheeled in for surgery praying Psalm 46:10: "Be still, and know that I am God." I didn't know what was ahead, but I knew I could trust that God would be there with me through it all.

Praying through Scripture can also help us align our prayers with God's will for us. First John 5:14–15 says, "This is the confidence we have in approaching God: that if we ask anything according to his will, he hears us." God's will is *not* a mystery; it's revealed to us in Scripture. When we pray God's Word, we're praying according to His will. For example, I've found myself praying, "Lord, You've promised that You have a plan for me, and You've said that when I seek You with all my heart, I will find You. So, today, I seek You first" (Jeremiah 29:11-14). When

I pray scriptures like that, I am aligning my desires with His will for my life. I'm building my life on a solid foundation by building my prayers on the truth of His Word.

Praying Scripture also helps us tap into the *power* of God's Word. When we pray Scripture, we're not just speaking human words; we're invoking God's living, active Word. And His Word carries divine power. It accomplishes what He desires. Remember that even Jesus, when He was tempted by Satan in the wilderness, instead of responding with His own words, used Scripture to counter the Enemy's lies. In Matthew 4, He quoted Deuteronomy 8:3 in response to temptation: "Man shall not live on bread alone, but on every word that comes from the mouth of God" (Matt. 4:4). When we pray Scripture, we're doing the same thing—we're speaking God's Word with authority, trusting that His Word will accomplish His purposes.

What if you made a habit of praying Scripture? How could it affect your life to use the Word of God to align your heart with His will, strengthen your faith, and tap into the power of His eternal Word? Whether we are facing anxiety, need guidance, or are seeking strength, God's Word can provide the very language we need when we pray. Praying verses from the Bible allows His living Word to shape our hearts, our prayers, and our lives. As Jesus said in Matthew 24:35, "Heaven and earth will pass away, but my words will never pass away." That is quite a promise to stand on! Next time you find yourself unsure of what to pray, reach for the Bible and remember: There's a verse for every situation!

"*Heaven*

AND *earth*

WILL PASS AWAY,

BUT MY WORDS

WILL *never*

PASS AWAY."

PRAYER CHALLENGE

Today, find a favorite scripture, especially one with a promise, and spend some time praying those words. Allow the truth of the Bible to guide you into deeper communion with God and into the trust and assurance that your prayers are aligned with His will.

PRAYER JOURNAL

1. Spend some time today writing down the challenges you are facing in your life. Then search the Bible for a scripture that relates to one of those challenges and write it down as well. For example, maybe you need to pray verses about God's provision; you could write out Philippians 4:19. Or maybe you need peace in your life today; write down John 14:27. When you finish this list, spend some time praying these verses and notice what God has to teach you.
2. How do you think praying Scripture can align your heart to God's will? Can you think of an example of that happening in your life?

chapter 13

WHERE TWO OR MORE ARE GATHERED

A few years ago a friend of our family suddenly fell ill and landed in intensive care. As his condition rapidly worsened, his wife called everyone together one evening for a prayer meeting, so everyone stopped what they were doing to gather. To see hundreds of people from our community show up and pack out the church to pray for healing was incredibly moving. I've heard the saying "There's power in numbers." This amazing scene of our community gathering reminded me of the strength that comes when believers get together for prayer. Moments like these make me think of when the disciples met up after Jesus' ascension. The very first thing they did was pray! "They all joined together constantly in prayer, along with the women and Mary the mother of Jesus, and with his brothers" (Acts 1:14).

Since that evening in 2020, I've felt compelled to dedicate more time at my concerts to prayer. My latest tour was called the Don't Stop Praying Tour, and throughout the concert we paused to pray between songs. Before the show, people were asked to write down prayer requests so that our team could pray for them. At one show a woman wrote to tell me that she was going in for cancer surgery the day after the concert, so we brought everyone together that night to pray over her. Carrying her crisis to the feet of Jesus as a community was by far my favorite moment of that evening. You know, I think that's what we do when we pray for (and with) one another. Whenever we gather to pray, we are like those followers in the gospel of Luke who had the faith to lower their paralytic friend down through the roof to the feet of Jesus.

When I was younger, I didn't always feel comfortable praying with others. I remember when I was growing up in church they would often kick off community prayer with the old "Everybody join hands." Now, that may be fine for most people, but I historically have really sweaty palms. Seriously, just the mention of "holding hands" would set off my anxiety when I was a kid. Even today, when someone so much as suggests joining hands in prayer, it seems like my palms immediately start to sweat!

Despite my fear of the whole hand-holding thing, I've come to realize that praying together is a powerful exercise that strengthens bonds and builds community. Prayer creates deep connectivity. I am here to tell you that prayer strengthens all our relationships. I've seen it happen. Have you heard the saying that "families who pray together stay together"? What if we started to believe that prayer is the mortar that holds us together—in our marriages, our families, our friendships, and our churches? Because I believe

I BELIEVE THAT PRAYING TOGETHER IS A *spark* THAT INVITES HEAVEN TO STEP INTO THE HERE AND NOW. IT IS AN *invitation* FOR JESUS TO CRASH THE PARTY.

a spiritual bond forms when we pray in community that deepens our relationships and connects us as believers.

Another one of the beautiful things I've noticed about the power of praying together is how it can bring people's guards down. When we pray together, we become more vulnerable. Sure, it can feel safer to be a loner, and our tendency might be to run from vulnerability with others, but opening up and praying with other people is not a sign of weakness. It is the key to a strong faith. I'm still learning all the ways that prayer is the core element of doing life together. I don't think Jesus ever meant for us to be lone-wolf Christians. But that's exactly what Satan wants. He wants us to be isolated. He wants us to avoid community. He wants to create distance between you and other believers because he knows that we are the body of Christ together. We need one another.

Jesus taught His disciples about the power of praying together: "Again, truly I tell you that if two of you on earth agree about anything they ask for, it will be done for them by my Father in heaven. For where two or three gather in my name, there am I with them" (Matt. 18:19–20). These verses point to something beautiful about agreement in prayer. Jesus was saying that there is significant power when two or more of us bring our hearts and voices into lockstep and focus on something together. We are syncing up our faith and trusting that He's listening and ready to move. I believe that praying together is a spark that invites heaven to

I believe a spiritual bond forms when we pray in community that deepens our relationships and connects us as believers.

step into the here and now. It is an invitation for Jesus to crash the party. And He promises to be right there, hanging out with us, when we call on Him together. What a beautiful picture of what it means to be the church: united in prayer, in agreement, and in faith. Where two or more of us are gathered in His name, He is there with us.

PRAYER CHALLENGE

Today's challenge is to gather your friends, your family, your spouse, or your small group and take some time to pray with other believers, even if you have to do it over Zoom or video call.

PRAYER JOURNAL

1. How often do you spend time praying with others? Is it a common practice in your life? Why or why not?
2. Can you find other examples in the Bible of believers gathering to pray? What happened?
3. How can praying together create bonds and bring down the guards, egos, and walls that often separate us from the people we love?

chapter **14**

BUILD DAILY PRAYER HABITS

I have learned that we are all intentional about the things that matter to us. I have a friend who is "intentional" about our local pro football team. He pays for season tickets, rents space for the tailgate, and even hits the extra-extra-early church service so he can get to the stadium to grill out ahead of kickoff on Sundays. It's a real commitment. I have another good friend who runs multiple marathons a year. When we go out for lunch, his menu choices are usually related to the miles he will have to run. He follows a strict training program so that he can finish each new race with a personal record. When he is training, all his life choices are built around finding success in the upcoming marathon. And I'm sure that you've heard all the latest morning-routine rages on social media. I've been trying some new daily routines, from ice baths to saunas, that are supposed to be good

"PICK A *place*,
HAVE A *plan*,
AND SET A *time*."

for my health. Of course, when I think about my daily routines and priorities, it makes me hyperaware of how easily we can order our days around so many things *other* than time spent talking to our heavenly Father!

Don't get me wrong—when it comes to prayer, I'm not saying it needs to be a morning routine. Any time is a good time to talk with God! Sometimes my day gets crazy, and my prayer time can get devoured by the chaos. But you know what I've found? Even if I miss the "ideal" moment, whenever I turn my thoughts to God, whether it's with a quick "Hey, thanks for this" or a "Lord, I need help here," it makes everything better. But I am also realizing that true spiritual growth happens when you make prayer a daily discipline. My pastor dropped some wisdom about prayer that stuck with me: "Pick a place, have a plan, and set a time." Simple, but so true.

Lately, I've been more intentional about guarding my morning prayer time. I'm telling you, when I start my day talking to God, it's like the whole atmosphere shifts. Prayer has this way of coloring everything else I do. Prayer affects how I move through my schedule, it sets me on a higher vantage point and allows me to see the eternal side of life's ups and downs, and it can even transform how I handle conflicts with people. It's wild to think it's the most life-giving discipline in my life, yet some days it is easier to jump into a forty-degree cold plunge than get still and take time to pray. Do you feel that same challenge with prayer?

Any time is a good time to talk with God!

That's why I love what the story of Daniel from the Old Testament has to teach me about praying. Yes, the same guy who survived the night in a den of hungry lions. The Bible tells us in the book of Daniel that even when a royal decree made it illegal to pray to God, Daniel still didn't flinch: "He went home to his upstairs room where the windows opened toward Jerusalem. Three times a day he got down on his knees and prayed, giving thanks to his God, just as he had done before" (6:10). Notice that Daniel had already developed the discipline of prayer time. So when trouble came calling, he called on God "just as he had done before." Whenever I am tempted to skip over prayer time, I think of Daniel, because that is a level of commitment I want to have. Three times a day! Daniel had a rhythm, a routine of seeking God, and he stuck to it no matter what was going on around him. Even hungry lions didn't scare him off his prayer routine.

It's pretty clear that we fill our days with the things that are a priority to us. The hard truth is that prayer time isn't just a daily choice—it's a reflection of our values. But we choose to pray, not because we *have* to, but because we *get* to! Just as Daniel did, we can build this habit into our daily lives, whether it is in the quiet of the morning, before every meal, or throughout our day. Building strong daily prayer habits starts with showing up, being consistent, and trusting that God is always right there waiting to meet us. At the end of the day, it's not just about a routine, it's about a relationship with the One who's always there waiting for me and ready to listen.

SHOW UP.

BE CONSISTENT.

Trust THAT GOD

IS ALWAYS

RIGHT THERE WAITING

TO MEET US.

PRAYER CHALLENGE

This week, set a timer on your phone or make a note in your planner to remind you to spend time praying at the same time each day. See how many consecutive days you can pray at these set times. After a few weeks you will have built talking to God into your daily routines!

PRAYER JOURNAL

1. What are some things that tend to get in the way of prayer time? What can you do to minimize these prayer blocks in your daily schedule?
2. Make a list of your daily routines (the things you are committed to each day). Which of these routines could you replace with prayer?
3. Write about the ways that a daily prayer routine can affect your life. Make a list of the things that could change if you were intentional about talking to God every day.

chapter 15

PRAYER IS A TIME TO LISTEN UP

Isn't it amazing how uncomfortable we are with just being quiet these days? We are so used to the surround sound of modern life that noise has become the norm. At least I know it has for me. Not long ago I had the chance to visit the Billy Graham Training Center in Asheville, North Carolina. I stayed at this place called the Cove for the evening. My hotel room was tucked away in the woods with no TV and no internet access. I remember sitting on the bed that night realizing that the first thing I do in any hotel room is turn on the TV, and the second thing I do is—yep—check my phone! That short stay in the quiet of the mountains highlighted just how much I've become uneasy with silence.

Lately, when I've found myself wondering *Is God speaking?* I've considered that maybe I should be asking myself a better question: *Am I listening?* I think we've all been around someone and thought, *That guy sure loves the sound of his own voice!* Ha! But so many of us are just uncomfortable with awkward pauses and complete quiet. I am learning that the noise surrounding me also seems to amplify the noise flowing through my inner world. Occasionally, when I am hanging out with my wife, she will ask, "Have you heard a single word I've said?" And I have to confess that my mind was off buzzing through tomorrow's work conversations and schedules. Honestly? I think God often wants to say the same thing to us: *Are you listening?*

I recently looked at the story of the prophet Elijah, who fled into the wilderness fearing for his life. The Bible says that God told Elijah to stand on a mountain and He would soon pass by (1 Kings 19:9–13). A mighty wind passed through the mountains, but God wasn't in the wind. An earthquake shook the ground, but God wasn't in the earthquake. A great fire blazed, but God wasn't in the fire. God wasn't found in the noisy, shock-and-awe kinds of moments. Nope. He showed up in a gentle whisper, a still, small voice. That story convicts me about God's tendency to speak gently and quietly when I am ready to listen.

I also love the verse we talked about in Mark that gives us a glimpse of Jesus' prayer life: "Very early in the morning, while it was still dark, Jesus got up, left the house and went off to a solitary place, where he prayed" (1:35). I don't know whether you have ever watched the series *The Chosen*, but it has plenty of scenes where the disciples are asking "Where is Jesus?" and He is off by Himself in prayer. Even in His busy ministry, Jesus made time for quiet moments with God. If Jesus needed solitude and quiet to connect with the Father, how much more do we?

"VERY EARLY IN
THE MORNING,
WHILE IT WAS STILL DARK,
JESUS GOT UP,
LEFT THE HOUSE AND
WENT OFF TO A
SOLITARY PLACE,
WHERE HE *prayed*"
(MARK 1:35).

I'll never forget the weeks that followed a vocal cord surgery that nearly ended my singing career when I literally couldn't voice a single word. During that season I really began to recognize how we're all so uncomfortable with silence. But that season of quiet became an incredible time of spiritual growth. I may have lost my voice, but I heard the voice of the Father like never before. And it made me crave more of that in my life. I get convicted sometimes about how often I still charge into the conversations with God when I should be listening. It might seem passive, but it requires digging in deeper and finding the quiet. I wonder how often we miss something special He is trying to say to us because we can't be quiet. What if God is just waiting for you to pause and listen today?

PRAYER CHALLENGE

Today, find a quiet place and pray this prayer: "Heavenly Father, help me to quiet my heart and listen for Your voice. In the busyness of life, remind me that You often speak in the stillness. Give me the wisdom to step away from distractions and spend time with You. Speak, Lord—I'm listening. Amen."

PRAYER JOURNAL

1. What distractions in your life keep you from listening to God?
2. How can you create more space for silence and stillness in your daily routine?
3. Think of a time when you felt God speaking to you, whether through Scripture, prayer, or a quiet moment. What did you learn from that experience, and how can you be more intentional about listening to Him now?

chapter **16**

PRAY WITHOUT CEASING

I have an important question for you: How many people in your life would answer the phone if you called them every hour on the hour? See whether you can think of one . . . I'll wait. This question reminds me of one of my favorite Christmas movies, *Elf*. (I've watched it with my girls so often I think I have every line memorized.) There's a scene in the movie after Buddy travels to New York and finds his dad, Walter Hobbs. Walter explains to Buddy that he has to go to the office for his workday, so he gives the very disappointed Buddy his work phone number with instructions to call if he needs anything. Walter has no idea what is coming next. Buddy doesn't know what to do with himself, so he calls his dad all day long. After a morning disrupted by these calls, and much to Walter's complete irritation because he is just trying to do his job, Buddy cheerfully hangs up, saying he'll call back again in five minutes. Makes me laugh every single time! How many people in your life would really be willing to answer your calls in the middle of a very busy day like that?

I've been considering this in the context of prayer and the truth that we can talk to God anytime, anywhere, in any situation, as often as we want, all day long. God is always there waiting for us to call on Him. (And I think God is probably a good bit busier managing the universe than Buddy's dad.) I think God not only "picks up" every time we pray but also delights in hearing the sound of His children's voices. I've always loved that old hymn "What a Friend We Have in Jesus" because it beautifully reminds us that He cares for every little detail of our lives. There is no friend like Jesus. We are invited to come to Him anytime, anyplace, and in every situation!

The apostle Paul wrote in 1 Thessalonians 5:16–18 that we should "rejoice always, pray without ceasing, give thanks in all circumstances; for this is the will of God in Christ Jesus for you" (ESV). Paul equated a spirit of joy and gratitude with the practice of prayer. God is always there for us, but what does it mean to pray without ceasing? For me, that kind of sounds impossible. I've always thought "Pray without ceasing" was one of those Bible sentiments that no one could ever actually do! But I am learning that it doesn't mean abandoning our responsibilities in order to pray all day. Instead, it's about inviting God into every detail of our daily lives.

I know my heart and mind are prone to wander, but in those moments when I whisper a prayer, God draws me back toward His will. He reminds me in those moments that I am not doing life alone. When we pray without ceasing, it becomes a constant, moment-to-moment invitation to connect with Him and

WE ARE *invited*

TO COME TO HIM:

Anytime.

Any place.

EVERY SITUATION!

listen to His voice. Prayer is a conversation, not a monologue. Paul's teaching about prayer takes me back to the first chapters of Genesis, where we see a beautiful picture of intimacy with God. The Bible tells us that Adam and Eve walked and talked with God in the "cool of the day" (Gen. 3:8). They didn't need to separate themselves for a formal prayer time or even stop what they were doing; their lives were marked by a natural, ongoing conversation with their Creator. This continual fellowship with God was woven into the fabric of their daily lives; walking and talking with God was as natural as breathing. Isn't that amazing?

Paul's insistence that we "pray without ceasing" echoes this desire for continuous fellowship with God. Just as Adam and Eve experienced unbroken communion with God, we are invited to live in a constant conversation with our Creator, who loves us. I think we are supposed to cultivate a life in which prayer is not just an isolated activity but a way of moving through the world. Whether we are working, resting, or interacting with others, to pray without ceasing means to be connected to God in every moment. We can imagine that we are walking with Him throughout our day—because we are! We can call to Him anytime, as much as we want, in every situation, to seek His guidance. And when we pray without ceasing, our thoughts, actions, and words are shaped by Him. I think moving through our days in this prayerful way brings us closer to the kind of intimate communion with God that Adam and Eve once knew in the garden.

PRAYER CHALLENGE

Every time you take a walk today, whether you are walking outside, walking through the hallway at school, walking to the break room, or heading into a meeting, take those few moments to talk to God.

PRAYER JOURNAL

1. Reflect on whether prayer feels more like a structured activity or an ongoing conversation with God. How would you like that to change?
2. Think of a time when you felt a strong connection to God. What were you doing, thinking, or feeling during that time? How can you cultivate that kind of awareness of God's presence throughout your day?
3. What might it look like for you personally to "pray without ceasing"? Are there specific moments in your day when you could invite God into your thoughts and actions more intentionally?
4. In what areas of your life do you struggle to remember God's presence? How can you use simple prayers or reminders to stay connected to God in those moments?

chapter 17

PRAYER IS AN ACTION

Our world often sees *pray* as a passive verb, as though it's not really doing anything. In our current popular culture, God is often left out of the story, and the idea that prayer could lead to material change gets ignored, dismissed, and even criticized. We shouldn't be surprised. Why would someone who hasn't experienced Jesus believe that prayer matters? You hear it all the time; after wildfires in California, floods in North Carolina, wars, or horrific shootings, someone on television or social media will yell, "Thoughts and prayers are not enough!" And I get it. There's frustration and misunderstanding behind that sentiment. But what challenges me most is this question: Do we as Christians believe prayer is an action? Do we live like it? Because if we don't think our prayers influence how God moves in the world, maybe we need to take a step back and ask ourselves some hard questions about our faith.

John Wesley, the British theologian and social reformer from the 1800s (he also founded the Methodist Church), once said something along the lines of, "God does nothing except in response to believing prayer." I love that sentiment. And if that's true, then prayer is never passive; it's powerful. *Pray* is an action verb. And if our prayers move the heart of God, then prayer is how we participate in what He's doing.

This reminds me of a great scene in the classic basketball movie *Hoosiers*. Gene Hackman's character, who is the head coach of the small Indiana high school team, tells Strap, the pastor's son, to come off the bench and check into a tense game. Right there in the middle of a packed gym, Strap kneels to pray while his teammates wait and everyone watches. The ref blows the whistle for play to resume and Strap just keeps praying. Finally, the coach taps him on the shoulder and says, "Strap, God wants you on the floor." Of course, Strap goes out and plays the best game of his life! It's funny, but it's also kind of true to life because prayer isn't a delay to action, it's what prepares us for it.

What if we lived like we really believe that? What if we stopped seeing prayer as something we squeeze in and instead viewed it as the catalyst for everything that matters in our lives and in the kingdom of God? I know of a surgeon who travels with a mission team to provide lifesaving operations in countries where people have no access to them. Every morning, before a single patient is prepped, he prays about each surgery, asking God for wisdom, steady hands, and the presence of the Great Physician in the operating room with him. That's prayer

Do we as Christians believe prayer is an action?

as action. That's what it looks like to believe prayer matters as much as the work itself.

Here's the bigger challenge: What if we prayed like that in every situation? What if we believed that praying for someone was just as important as tangibly helping them? Because Scripture tells us that it is just as powerful. Look at Jesus as He stood at Lazarus's tomb ready to raise him from the dead. What did He do first? He prayed: "Father, I thank you that you have heard me. I knew that you always hear me" (John 11:41–42). If prayer was an action to Jesus, surely it is that for us as well.

Prayer is the action of surrender to God. It's an action of recognizing our dependence on the One from whom true provision comes. And prayer doesn't just prepare us for action; it also compels us to act in the world. If you don't believe me, pray for someone consistently and see how it changes the way you interact with and serve that person! I don't think popular culture will ever embrace it, but I don't want to dismiss prayer as passive in my daily life. I want to embrace the truth that when we pray, we are inviting the God of the universe to move before we step into action. Just as Strap did before he ran onto the basketball court. And just as the surgeon who prays before each surgery does. I want us to embrace the biblical truth that prayer is the first action. Let's live like it.

Prayer isn't a delay to action, it's what prepares us for it.

PRAYER CHALLENGE

Think of one situation in your life where you're seeking change or a breakthrough. Take some time today to actively pray over it and then follow up on that prayer time by taking a step forward in faith.

PRAYER JOURNAL

1. Do you believe that prayer is an action? Reflect on times in your life when you turned to prayer, especially in moments of crisis or uncertainty.
2. How might your perspective shift if you saw prayer as the first step in partnering with God to bring change?
3. How does your daily life reflect your belief in the power of prayer? Is prayer a reaction or a starting point? Journal about one area in your life where you could intentionally invite God in through prayer, not just for strength, but for guidance and purpose.

chapter **18**

YES, PRAYER IS WAR

Jesus didn't sugarcoat the great divide between His hopes for us and what the devil intends for our lives. He referenced it throughout His teachings: "The thief comes only to steal and kill and destroy; I have come that they may have life, and have it to the full" (John 10:10). In that verse, He was drawing a line in the sand about the reality of the cosmic struggle we've been thrown into. There's an Enemy of your soul, and he has nothing but very bad intentions for every relationship, hope, dream, and endeavor in your life. But Jesus has a magnificent plan for you; He calls it "life to the fullest." Given the stark reality of Jesus' words, we can't afford to forget that we find ourselves in the middle of this spiritual battle and we have to choose sides. And prayer is not just a comforting conversation with God. It's how we join the fight.

I don't know about you, but I don't always recognize that underneath everything going on in my life is an intense spiritual war for my soul and the souls of everyone I meet. And the moment I forget that I am waking up and stepping into a battlefield, well, that is the moment I forget to put on my armor. Maybe you feel like this, too, but I too often walk into life's spiritual battles wearing flip-flops, and then I end up wondering why my soul feels beaten down by lunchtime. The apostle Paul wrote in Ephesians 6 that no matter what else we think is going on, we should be prepared to fight: "Put on the full armor of God, so that you can take your stand against the devil's schemes. . . . And pray in the Spirit on all occasions with all kinds of prayers and requests" (vv. 11, 18).

Prayer is not just a comforting conversation with God. It's how we join the fight.

Maybe you remember singing this old song in Sunday school: "I may never march in the infantry, ride in the cavalry, shoot the artillery; I may never fly o'er the enemy, but I'm in the Lord's army—yes, sir!" It was cute when we were kids, marching around the church basement pretending to be soldiers. But Paul wasn't talking about playing dress-up. He was serious. He understood what was at stake. And he didn't just list out the armor of truth, righteousness, peace, faith. He also ended with prayer. That's right—prayer is how we wear our armor. It's how we stay connected to God in the fight for eternity.

So let me ask you: How aware are you of the spiritual warfare going on around you each day? The battle isn't always obvious. It doesn't always look like temptation or tragedy. Sometimes it's discouragement. Sometimes it's a distraction or that subtle voice of doubt in the middle of an ordinary day. The battlefield isn't always the loud conflict. Sometimes it's in the quiet of your car at the end of a stressful day when you find yourself whispering desperate prayers. Sometimes it's in the still of the night, as fresh tears of worry stream down for a loved one. That's where the fight is happening, and our God is there with us. But Paul also taught us that we don't approach the fight the same way the world does. "For though we live in the world, we do not wage war as the world does. The weapons we fight with are not the weapons of the world" (2 Cor. 10:3–4). Prayer and truth are spiritual weapons with divine power to shatter the Enemy's strongholds.

Scripture's encouragement to view prayer as our weapon is the proof that we are not fighting alone. We pray because we know we can't fight this fight on our own and because we know we don't have to. Exodus 14:14 gives us this promise: "The Lord will fight for you; you need only to be still." That verse stops me in my tracks, because I'm a fighter by nature. If you know me, you know I want to jump in, fix things, solve problems, and defend myself or my loved ones if I have to. When we pray, we aren't waving a white flag, we're lifting our hearts in surrender and joining the fight with the God who's already won this cosmic war.

The Enemy is after our families, our peace, our identites, and our souls. But prayer pushes back the darkness and invites God into the action. When we lift our voices in prayer, we step into the battle to say "Not today, Satan." Prayer is how we fight for our marriages. It's how we battle for our kids, our churches, our friends, our calling. When we pray for others, we join God

HOW AWARE ARE YOU OF

THE *spiritual warfare*

GOING ON AROUND

YOU EACH DAY?

in His rescue mission. I believe that every time we choose prayer over panic and worship instead of worry, we're reminding the Enemy that we belong to Jesus. And there is nothing that terrifies that thief more than our Lord and Savior. Prayer is where our weak words become powerful, because they're held in the hands of a mighty God. So, today, suit up in that armor. Stand firm, even in the moments when life feels uncertain, and pray like it matters, because it does.

PRAYER CHALLENGE

Where do you sense the battle in your life right now? Take time to name the areas in your life where you feel pressure, temptation, discouragement, or distraction, and ask God to fight those spiritual battles for you. "Lord, open my eyes to see where the Enemy may be trying to steal, kill, or destroy. Help me stand firm and fight with Your strength."

PRAYER JOURNAL

1. Read through Ephesians 6:10–18 and reflect on each piece of the armor of God. Write about the areas where you may need God to help you "suit up" today.
2. Think back on a time when prayer made a real difference, when it changed your perspective, brought a breakthrough, or gave you peace in a hard moment. Write out the story and consider how that memory shapes the way you join the spiritual battle with prayer.

chapter 19

PRAY FOR YOUR ENEMIES

I'll just be real with you. This is a topic I didn't look forward to writing about. Out of all the ways we talk about prayer, this one feels like a bigger challenge to me. I didn't even want to start typing this because I already felt convicted the moment I opened my Bible and began to study. The idea of praying for my enemies usually leaves me thinking, *God, isn't it hard enough to forgive them? And now You want me to pray for them too?* Maybe you can relate to that sentiment. And just as I sit writing this, I realize how I might struggle to pray for the guy who cut me off in traffic this morning. Ha!

In Matthew, Jesus didn't leave much wiggle room for misinterpretation: "You have heard that it was said, 'Love your neighbor and hate your enemy.' But I tell you, love your enemies and pray for those who persecute you, that you may be children of your Father in heaven" (5:43–45). To follow Jesus is to love your enemies *and* pray for them! Not roll your eyes at them, or gossip about them, or hit "unfollow" on their social media because they have different views from yours. Nope, we are to *pray* for them.

In Southern culture there is a little phrase that sounds like a prayer but definitely isn't: "Bless their heart." Let me translate for you if you live up north: "That person is a mess." "Bless their heart" sounds sweet, but we all know it's a polite way of putting down those enemy types in our lives. Jesus calls us to something much deeper and more difficult, to something holy. Look at what He did on the cross. Jesus, in unspeakable pain, looked down at the people who had betrayed Him, beat Him, spit on Him, and nailed His hands and feet, and at many who were mocking Him in that very moment, and He said, "Father, forgive them, for they know not what they do" (Luke 23:34 ESV). Wow! That moment in the Bible gets me every time I read it. If Jesus could pray for His enemies while bleeding out and taking His last breaths on the execution stand for their salvation, surely I can learn to pray for my own difficult people.

To follow Jesus is to love your enemies *and* pray for them!

I think it's important to talk about the word *enemies* for a minute before we move on. We just don't use that particular term often outside war movies or unhinged political rants. But if we're honest, we've all got a list of enemies. We call them by different names, though: the coworker who competes with you at every turn, the neighbor who seems to enjoy being difficult, the ex who wounded you, the former friend who ghosted you, the person who betrayed your trust, and, yes, the one with the other party's political bumper sticker.

But let's not pretend it's easy to pray for our enemies, because it isn't. I once had a major business deal go sideways because of someone's deceit. It wasn't just one bad moment—it was betrayal, sleepless nights, stress, and even countless hours in a courtroom that I never dreamed would be a reality of my life. And let me tell you, the very last thing I wanted to do was pray for the person responsible for this mess. What I hoped for a lot of days was to find that one Bible verse in my morning devotional time that would let me pray something like "Dear Lord, let him see that I'm right and he's wrong," or maybe something Old Testament–style: "Smite him with holy fire or turn him into a pillar of salt." (Ha! Just being honest.) But you know what? Jesus doesn't play that game. He doesn't give us an out. He just commands us, "Pray for them." Talk about a command that works on your soul in tough situations.

But here's the secret I've learned from some wise older believers: It is nearly impossible to stay bitter toward someone you're genuinely praying for. You can't keep clinging to a grudge when you're lifting that person before God in prayer and petition. Something happens in you when you pray for someone you see as an enemy. God starts to change your perspective. You stop seeing that person as the bad guy and start seeing him or her as a wounded, misguided person who is a child of God . . . just like you.

Let me be very clear: Jesus wouldn't ask you to put yourself back in harm's way. If you're in an abusive or dangerous relationship, this is not a call to remain silent or passive. Boundaries are holy, and your safety matters. Jesus calls us to pray with love in

WHEN'S THE LAST TIME YOU *prayed* FOR SOMEONE WHO HURT YOU, *disagreed* WITH YOU, OR MADE YOUR LIFE *difficult*?

our hearts, even from a distance, even when our emotions haven't caught up yet. And you know what? Here is the craziest part: Prayer doesn't change just you; it might also change them. When you pray for that person you're at odds with, God can do something on both sides of the line. He can soften that person's heart too. He can restore what was broken and rewrite your story.

Here's the gut-check question I keep coming back to, the one that forced me to take a long look in the spiritual mirror as I sat down to write about this particular truth: When's the last time you prayed for someone who hurt you, disagreed with you, or made your life difficult? If your answer is "Not in a long time," you're not alone. Jesus calls us to pray for our enemies because, ultimately, this isn't about them—it's about becoming more like Him. Today, I will take a deep breath and ask God for the strength to do what sometimes feels impossible. I'm going to start praying for my enemies—not the "Bless their heart" kind of prayer, but a grace-filled, honest, courageous prayer. I want to challenge you to join me. Even if you don't feel like it, pray anyway and let God do the rest.

PRAYER CHALLENGE

Beginning today, take Jesus at His word and pray intentionally for someone who has hurt you, frustrated you, or disagreed with you, or who even feels like an enemy in your life. Start with one person. Write down his or her name. Ask God for the strength to pray sincerely, even if your heart isn't there yet.

PRAYER JOURNAL

1. How does Jesus' example on the cross challenge your natural response to conflict, offense, or betrayal? What would it look like to respond more like Him in your own relationships?
2. Think about that person in your life who feels the hardest to pray for right now—write about what emotions or memories come up when you think about this person and how you can give that to God.
3. Write about several ways you think prayer could shift your perspective toward difficult people in your life and open the door to healing.

chapter 20

PRAY FOR THE IMPOSSIBLE

We serve a miracle-working God. I know that's a bold statement in a world that doesn't talk much about miracles, but if we're talking about prayer, *really* talking about prayer, we have to be willing to pray for the impossible. Not just the everyday, ordinary things (though those matter too), but we are called to pray for the stuff that looks beyond all hope, that leaves us feeling desperate, the situations where we have no plan B. We are called to pray in those "it's gonna take a miracle" moments. We have to embrace praying for the impossible.

> We have to embrace praying for the impossible.

It too often feels like the miracles we read about in the Bible belong to some other era. Like all the miracles ended when the last words of the New Testament were written. A scroll through today's news is a quick reminder: It is full of fear, division, and bad headlines. And as you walk through your day today, maybe you've started wondering where the God who parted seas, raised the dead, and fed five thousand with a few loaves and fish has gone?

The really good news is that He hasn't changed. The same God who split the Red Sea still hears the cries of His people. The God who made water flow from a rock in the middle of the wilderness still provides for us in dry places of life. The God who led His people with a cloud by day and a pillar of fire at night is still showing up today to lead us—in ways we don't always expect. Miracles aren't just ancient museum pieces; they are still happening all around us. I've been challenging myself lately to pray like I believe that truth!

I wrote a song once about my friend William who is a living, breathing miracle. When he was just a baby, he suffered a series of severe strokes. The doctors told his parents he'd never walk, never talk, never live a "normal" life. But God had a different plan. Fast-forward to age thirteen, when William stood onstage at his home church on Easter Sunday, sharing his story and running around the sanctuary to celebrate exactly what the doctors said would never happen. And that wasn't the end of his miracle. The last time I talked with William—this boy who wasn't supposed to ever speak—and his family, they said he is now in law school in New Mexico, training to stand in courtrooms and communicate with power and clarity on behalf of others. That's a miracle—no doubt about it.

Let me ask you to consider something today. What are you afraid to pray for because it feels too big, too far gone, too lost, or too broken? What have you quietly stopped hoping for because it seems so impossible? If you follow Jesus, you're called to be someone who believes in miracles. Disciples of Jesus are people who stare down mountains and say "Move!" Jesus taught His followers, "Truly I tell you, if anyone says to this mountain, 'Go, throw yourself into the sea,' and does not doubt in their heart but believes that what they say will happen, it will be done for them'" (Mark 11:23). That verse isn't just a poetic metaphor—it's a call to live a bold, faithful life of prayer.

And don't think for a second that God works only in the dramatics of parted seas and crumbling walls. Sometimes miracles happen quietly, right in your living room. As with my friend whose post-surgery infection nearly took his life. His wife felt led to pray for him one night, and during that short prayer they noticed something that sent them to the hospital just in time. The doctors said that if they had waited just a few more hours, an infection would have reached his heart. That quiet living-room prayer saved his life—that's a miracle.

There are moments in life when we hit a wall of hopelessness. When we've exhausted every resource, every plan, and every strategy. But what I have learned is that's often the very place where we find the God of the breakthrough waiting. Sometimes it takes being broken for us to finally reach out to Him in faith. There's a powerful story in Mark 5 about a woman who had been bleeding for twelve years. Twelve. That's a long time to hurt, to hope, to be disappointed. She'd spent everything she had on doctors, but instead of getting better, she got worse. Maybe you've been there. Maybe you know someone like this. Maybe you're in a similarly hopeless situation right now.

The Bible says, "When she heard about Jesus, she came up

WE PRAY BECAUSE GOD HEARS US. WE PRAY BECAUSE WE BELIEVE GOD

still HEALS,

still PROVIDES,

still BREAKS CHAINS,

AND *still* OPENS TOMBS.

behind him in the crowd and touched his cloak, because she thought, 'If I just touch his clothes, I will be healed'" (Mark 5:27–28). That's all the faith she had left—just enough to stretch out her hand and touch the edge of His robe. And that was enough. Jesus turned, found her in the crowd, and spoke these words: "Daughter, your faith has healed you. Go in peace and be freed from your suffering" (v. 34). Can you imagine that moment of healing? I wonder what it would look like to bring that level of surrender and faith to my prayer life. To reach out for Jesus with the impossible.

What's your twelve-year prayer? What's the thing you've cried about, journaled about, maybe even given up on? Don't stop praying for it. Reach out again—even if it's just a whisper of hope left. We pray because God hears us. We pray because we believe God *still* heals, *still* provides, *still* breaks chains, and *still* opens tombs. So let me say it again: Following Jesus means that we pray for the impossible.

> We pray for the child who's wandered from faith.
> We pray for the diagnosis that doesn't look good.
> We pray for the marriage that's hanging by a thread.
> We pray for the friend who doesn't believe.
> We pray for our own hearts to be set on fire again.

When doubt and hopelessness creep into your life and you are tempted to think God doesn't do that kind of thing anymore, I want you to remind yourself that He never stopped. Let's hold tight to the truth that Jesus taught us in the gospel of Matthew: "With man this is impossible, but with God all things are possible" (19:26).

PRAYER CHALLENGE

This week, take a bold step of faith and pray specifically for something that feels impossible. Write it down, speak it out loud, and keep asking, even if nothing changes right away. Trust that your miracle could be just one prayer away.

PRAYER JOURNAL

1. What's one situation in your life right now that feels impossible? Name it honestly. Have you been praying about it—or have you given up hope?
2. When was the last time you witnessed or experienced something you would call a miracle?
3. How did it affect your faith?
4. Do you find it hard to believe that God still does the miraculous today? Why or why not?
5. Like the woman in Mark 5, what step of faith could you take this week to reach out to Jesus with your need? What does that look like practically for you?

chapter 21

PRAYERS OF THANKSGIVING

One of the biggest game-changers in the life of faith is learning how to begin prayer time with gratitude. I'm not just talking about throwing out the casual "Thanks, God" before moving on to a long list of needs; I mean learning to begin prayer with a deep, rooted, perspective-shifting thanksgiving—the kind that transforms the way we live and how we view everything around us. Recently, I traveled to Hawaii with my family and experienced a deeply transformational moment I'll never forget.

One evening we were with a small group who were worshiping, and they began singing "The Doxology." You know the one: "Praise God from whom all blessings flow; praise Him, all creatures here below; praise Him above, ye heavenly host . . ." And as the harmonies carried through the air, I looked around at the ocean, the mountains, my healthy family all together—and it took me to church!

That one little song sparked a moment of awareness and ushered in a tidal wave of gratitude. I wasn't asking God for anything; I was simply overwhelmed by how good He is and how thankful I am for every little blessing in my life, because it all comes from Him. And let me tell you, it changed everything about that trip for me. That's the power of gratitude and thanksgiving. It's hard to complain about the world when you're standing in awe of the One who created it. It's even harder to stay discouraged when you're counting all the ways He's blessed you.

I've met a lot of folks who walk through hard seasons and still choose joy. Many of them have experienced loss or pain, but they've also seen God show up in ways they'll never forget. They don't take a sunrise for granted. They don't miss a chance to give thanks. But we shouldn't have to hit rock bottom to recognize how blessed we are. What if we chose gratitude every day, even in those moments when life felt just okay? What if we started each and every prayer with words of thanksgiving—before the miracle, before the healing, before the breakthrough? Jesus did exactly that.

Before feeding the five thousand, Jesus didn't panic about the small lunch in front of Him. He didn't focus on the huge crowd or the lack of anything more than a few loaves and fish. *He gave thanks.* "Jesus then took the loaves, gave thanks, and distributed to those who were seated as much as they wanted" (John 6:11). It is powerful to recognize that the miracle followed gratitude and not the other way around. Jesus thanked God for what He had *before* it was multiplied. I think that tells us something important. Gratitude isn't about the size of the blessing; it's about the size of the God we're trusting. The Psalms of the Old Testament are overflowing with this kind of thanksgiving: "Enter his gates

“ENTER HIS GATES WITH

thanksgiving

AND HIS COURTS

WITH *praise*;

GIVE THANKS TO HIM AND

praise HIS NAME”

(PS. 100:4).

with thanksgiving and his courts with praise; give thanks to him and praise his name" (Ps. 100:4). Even the early church caught this rhythm. Acts is filled with moments when gratitude became the fuel for faith. When Paul and Silas were beaten and thrown into prison, they didn't whine; they lifted up prayers of praise and thanksgiving in the middle of their pain.

I often need the reminder I've learned that when I lead with thanksgiving in prayer, everything else follows. My worries shrink, my bitterness softens, and my joy returns. Gratitude grounds me in the goodness of God and reminds me that no matter what I'm facing, He's still faithful. So lately I've tried to write down three things I'm thankful for every day and turn them into a short prayer. It might sound simple, but it's helped me see the blessings I used to overlook. And, more than that, it's helped me focus my heart on the Giver behind all of life's gifts. Whether it's taking a beautiful morning walk, hearing a kind word from a friend, or just being part of "the wake-up club," those small thanksgivings shift my perspective. So even if you're walking through something hard right now, let me encourage you to start your prayers with thanksgiving. Don't wait for everything to be perfect. Just begin with one good thing—even the smallest thing—and bring it to God. Because when we with gratitude remember what He's already done, our hearts open wide to believe in what He will do next.

PRAYER CHALLENGE

Take a few minutes today to write down three things you're thankful for. Whether they are big or small, name them specifically. Turn that list into a prayer of thanksgiving. Try this each day for the next week and watch how it transforms your heart, your conversations with God, and even your outlook on life.

PRAYER JOURNAL

1. When do you tend to overlook things you should be grateful for? How can you change that?
2. When was the last time gratitude changed your attitude or outlook in a difficult moment? Describe what happened and how it affected your prayer life.
3. Is there an area in your life where you've been more focused on what's missing than what's been given? How could beginning your prayers with thanksgiving reshape that situation?

chapter 22

PRAYERS FOR COURAGE

Have you ever prayed a prayer like this? "God, help me have my eyes open for opportunities to share my faith." It can be a dangerous prayer, not because it's wrong, but because it's one prayer you can be sure that God will answer! When you start praying courageous prayers, don't be surprised if He places you right in the middle of an opportunity to use that courage. The truth is that courage doesn't always look like speaking truth to power, facing down a den full of lions, or charging into the Red Sea. Sometimes courage is raising your hand to volunteer, helping a homeless person you've never met, or speaking the name of Jesus in a room where it might cost you something. I've been thinking a lot about the people who make up what I like to call the Faith Hall of Fame. You know those courageous heroes of the Bible who laid down their comfort, their safety, and even their lives for the sake of the gospel? They didn't get there by accident—they did it with prayer. Because true courage starts with a simple, honest request: "God, help me be bold."

Recently, my daughter Lulu told me she wanted to go on a mission trip to the ends of the earth. She wants people to know Jesus and felt called to take that message far beyond her comfort zone. That conversation humbled me. I mean, what a powerful thing to witness your child saying yes to God with that kind of courage. And there's my friend Daniel McCloud, who shared his story on my podcast. It's one I won't soon forget, because of the impact it is having here in my hometown. Back in high school he had this fire in his heart to share Jesus. That passion sparked a revival at his school. Fast-forward a few years, and Daniel is leading a ministry right in the heart of Nashville—on lower Broadway, of all places. If you've ever been there on a weekend night, you know it's way more of a party zone than a prayer meeting. But Daniel and his team walk into that chaos and offer prayers, conversations, and the hope of Jesus to people from all over the world.

These examples make me consider what courage looks like in my own life. Am I willing to pray for courage—even if it costs me? The disciples knew what it meant to follow Jesus with everything. In the New Testament, following Him meant walking away from their boats, their businesses, their families, and everything in their lives that felt secure. They didn't just dip one toe in the water—they jumped out of the boat with both feet. Just like Peter. Remember how he saw Jesus

Am I willing to pray for courage—even if it costs me?

walking on the water and said, "Lord, if it's you . . . tell me to come to you on the water" (Matt. 14:28)? Jesus did, and Peter stepped out of the boat. For a moment, as he kept his eyes on Jesus, he walked on the water just like the Teacher. But fear crept in and Peter started to sink. That's the visual I come back to when I think about praying for courage. It's not a one-and-done kind of practice. It's a daily rhythm of stepping out in courage, praying again for more courage. Courage, it turns out, looks a lot like baby steps. And each one is kept afloat by prayer.

There's this idea that courage means never feeling fear, but I don't think that's true. I think courage and fear can show up at the same time—and that's why we pray. Because we're not tapping into some internal self-made bravery but leaning on God's strength to do what we can't do on our own. When we pray for courage, we're inviting God to lead us into something bigger than ourselves. And when God calls you to something, He's already factored in your fear, your hesitation, your shortcomings, and your doubt. He knows everything you need to accomplish His will. What is that boat in your life you need the courage to step out of? I want to challenge you to remember that it takes one prayer for courage to take one step of faith. But a prayer and a step lead to another prayer and another step, and before you know it, you're walking on water.

PRAYER CHALLENGE

This week, pray a simple but dangerous prayer: "God, give me courage." Ask Him to open your eyes to opportunities where you can share your faith, show love, or step outside your comfort zone. Then be ready, because the opportunity might come in a conversation, a decision, or a moment when you'd rather stay silent.

PRAYER JOURNAL

1. When was a time you felt God nudging you to do something courageous, but you hesitated? What held you back, and what do you think might help you respond differently next time?
2. Who in your life inspires you with their courageous faith? What specifically about their story or choices encourages you to be bold in your own journey?
3. What are some "boats" you might be clinging to instead of stepping out in faith like Peter did? Is there something you need to leave behind to follow Jesus more fully?

chapter 23

PRAYERS OF IDENTITY

Every time we pray, we enter into a sacred conversation with the One who made us. Think about that for a moment. We, the created, get the full attention of the Creator. And when we pray, we are reminded of something the world is quick to make us forget: our truest identity. The world tries to give you a thousand other answers to the question of your identity. According to the world, you're only as good as your last performance. You're worth only as much as your paycheck or the zip code you live in. You're valuable only if you're noticed or if you have a million followers on social media. So it can be easy to lose track of who God made you to be when the world is constantly offering you identity detours.

I once wrote a song called "Hello, My Name Is," inspired by a guy named Jordan. He was a standout athlete, a big personality at his school. But after a series of sports injuries, his life began to unravel. He got tangled up in addiction, and somewhere along the way he started believing he was an addict, a failure, a lost cause. But God had better plans. He reminded Jordan of his true identity and changed his life, and Jordan changed a lot of other lives for the better. At concerts for that tour, we'd hand out poster-sized name tags and invite people to write down the false names the world had given them—names like "rejected," "not enough," "mistake," "invisible." Then we'd spend time in prayer inviting God to replace those lies with the truth. The response was incredible. We would write words like "loved," "redeemed," and "child of God," and you could see transformation happening in people's lives.

I'll be honest—I can't tell you how many times in my job I can get caught chasing the wrong version of identity. I look at the plaques on my studio wall as I write this and think, *Is this what defines me?* I've spent a lot of time trying to make a name for myself. I know better. While there's nothing wrong with working hard or creating something you're proud of, none of it—not the music, not the success, not the applause—can tell me who I *really* am. But it seems as though we are all looking for identity everywhere but the Source, and it starts at a young age. I remember as a kid I loved wearing my baseball uniform. That jersey felt like my name tag. People knew me as "the baseball guy," and I liked that. I clung to it. And when it became clear that my dreams of playing first base for the Chicago Cubs weren't realistic, I had to figure out the question *If I'm not a baseball player, then who am I?*

As we get older, identity becomes a serious question a lot of us wrestle with. We are easily drawn to identities based on what sets us apart from others—awards, straight A's, championships, applause. But while the world tells us to build our identities, God invites us to receive our identities. That's where prayer becomes so key. When we come to God in prayer, we're not performing. We're not hustling. We're not earning a title. We're coming home. We're remembering who we are and *whose* we are.

A friend of mine tells a story that illustrates why we struggle with identity. He was trying to give away a nice couch at his yard sale, so he put a sign on it that read "Free to a good home." Dozens of people walked by this really nice couch and shook their heads. Some even asked him suspiciously what was wrong with it. Finally, frustrated, he changed the sign to read "$50." The very next person who walked into his sale bought it without hesitation. People are suspicious of free things. But isn't that how we treat God's grace and His identity for us? We feel like we have to hustle, impress, and separate ourselves from others to earn what God has already given us. But our truest self—our identity—isn't something we earn. It's a gift. Paid for by Jesus and offered freely.

Your identity in Him is unshakable and unchanging. The Bible tells you that you are not your title, you are not your worst or best moment, you are especially not your most viewed Instagram reel. It says that you and I are "a chosen people, a royal priesthood, a holy nation, God's special possession" (1 Peter 2:9). And the verse ends saying we were called from darkness into light so we can declare God's praises. That's *identity* with a purpose. So the next time the world tries to rename you, the next time your failures or your fears start talking louder than God's promises, I challenge you to pray, "Lord, remind me who I really am." Staying close to your Creator is the only way to fully embrace your true identity as a child of the one true King!

"LORD,

remind

ME WHO I

REALLY AM."

PRAYER CHALLENGE

Each day this week, take a moment to sit quietly in prayer and ask God to remind you of who you are in Him. Write down one identity statement from Scripture such as "I am God's workmanship" (Eph. 2:10) or "I am a child of God" (John 1:12).

PRAYER JOURNAL

1. What labels or false identities have you carried that don't line up with who God says you are? How have they shaped the way you see yourself?
2. When do you find yourself tempted to make a name for yourself instead of resting in your God-given identity?
3. What would change in your daily life if you fully embraced your identity as God's chosen, loved, and set-apart child?
4. Have you ever been surprised by how prayer reminded you of who you really are? Describe that moment and what you learned from it.

chapter 24

PRAY THE "WHY, GOD?" PRAYERS

There's one kind of prayer that all of us will eventually pray—no matter how strong our faith, how long we've followed Jesus, or how many times we've seen Him work miracles in our lives. I call it the "Why, God?" prayer. Maybe you know the one. Maybe you've prayed it at a hospital bedside, through tears on the steering wheel, or beside a casket that should've never been filled. Maybe you whispered it after a betrayal, a diagnosis, a tragedy that made absolutely no sense.

Why, God?

Why did my spouse walk out?

Why is my child battling addiction?

Why couldn't the cancer be healed? Or treated much closer to home?

Why did Amy have to bury her daughter, Brooke, after such a long battle?

Why did a shooting have to happen at Covenant School?

We don't like to talk about those prayers much, especially in a world that prefers easy answers and orderly faith. But these are the very kinds of prayers that King David, who the Bible says was a man after God's own heart, prayed often in the Psalms. These are the prayers that too often remind us just how human we are. They are prayers that matter because we know God isn't after polished words and perfect theology. He wants a relationship built on honesty. And the deepest, most sincere relationships are full of honest questions, raw questions, and sometimes angry, confused, grief-stricken questions. The good news, of course, is that our God can handle all our whys.

God already knows the other side of our "Why?" questions. And even when He doesn't answer the way we hope, He always offers His presence, His nearness, and His love. The Psalms are full of "Why, God?" prayers. King David asked it more than once: "Why, Lord, do you stand far off? Why do you hide yourself in times of trouble?" (Ps. 10:1) and "My God, my God, why have you forsaken me? Why are you so far from saving me, so far from my cries of anguish?" (22:1). Look, these aren't polite prayers the king of Israel was offering up. These are gut-wrenching prayers. And yet David didn't get struck by lightning for crying out. He wasn't silenced for screaming for answers. He received the space to be real with God. And slowly, through the course of these psalms, David always circled back to trust.

And then there's Jesus' friend Martha. When her brother Lazarus died, she met Jesus on the road and said, "Lord . . . if you had been here, my brother would not have died" (John 11:21).

HE ALWAYS OFFERS

HIS *presence*,

HIS *nearness*,

AND HIS *love*.

She believed in Jesus' power, but she didn't understand His timing; yet she still came to Him. It was grief wrapped in faith. She brought the question anyway. Remember that Jesus Himself asked "Why, God?" on the cross. In His most human moment, Jesus cried out, "My God, my God, why have you forsaken me?" (Matt. 27:46). If the Son of God could pray that prayer, then surely we're allowed to ask our own whys. And if you've read the end of the story, you know the answer didn't come in that Friday's moment of darkness; it came at sunrise on Sunday, when the stone was rolled away and death was defeated.

If you have kids, think about the kind of relationship you want to have with them. I've always wanted my daughters to know that they can come to me with anything. They don't have to clean it up or make sense of it first. I just want them to come and talk to me. Sometimes I have answers and sometimes I don't. Sometimes I just listen, and very often I am learning that the best thing I can offer them is a hug instead of an answer. But I want them to know that I am always available for them.

I think that's exactly how our heavenly Father feels about us. He doesn't shut us down. He doesn't roll His eyes at our questions. He invites us into the mystery, into the relationship, and into the kind of trust that doesn't require all the answers. I believe one day we'll see the whole picture. Until then, He meets us in the middle of the unknown. So go ahead and ask all your "Why?" questions, because God can handle them. And even if the only answer you get is the promise of His presence, that is more than enough.

PRAYER CHALLENGE

This week, take a few minutes each day to bring your "Why, God?" question to Him. Don't filter it or clean it up—just come as you are. Write it down or speak it out loud in your car or whisper it through your tears. Then sit in silence for a minute and ask God to meet you there.

PRAYER JOURNAL

1. What's one "Why, God?" prayer you've carried for a long time? Have you been avoiding it, or have you brought it to Him honestly?
2. How has God's presence comforted you in seasons when your "Why?" questions were hard to carry?
3. What does it mean to you that Jesus asked "Why?" on the cross? How does that change the way you approach your own difficult questions for God?
4. When you get to heaven, what's one question you know you'll want to ask? And how does trusting God now prepare your heart for then?

chapter 25

PRAYERS FOR BREAKING BREAD

If you've been to my house for a holiday, you've probably experienced the magic of my wife, Emily's, dinner table. She's what I like to call "the hostess with the mostest." She is always inviting, always including, always creating space for everyone to belong. At last year's Easter Sunday celebration, Emily invited a whole bunch of people and had our dining room set like something out of a magazine, with festive plates, centerpieces, and the part I always love most: the name cards. At first glance, those name cards near the place settings don't look like much in the grand scheme of things. But I think those little folded cards say something powerful. Each one communicates, "You belong here. We planned for you. We've been waiting for you."

Once everyone arrives around the table, Emily always asks me to say a prayer over dinner and our time together. And whenever we host a dinner like this, it never fails that by the end of the night, a table full of people who didn't know one another well (or even at all) walk out as friends. I think that's the beauty of breaking bread together, especially when the time is soaked in hospitality and prayer. Over the years I've come to realize that breaking bread and praying are not separate acts. When we pray before a meal, we're not just giving thanks for the food—we're acknowledging the sacredness of being together. We're slowing down, inviting God in, and turning an ordinary dinner table into holy ground.

Reading through the Bible, it becomes apparent that Jesus was always sitting down to eat with all kinds of people from all walks of life—tax collectors, disciples, sinners, religious leaders, and friends. The Gospels are filled with scenes around dinner tables, loaves of bread, shared wine, and important words over meals. The most profound moment happened in the upper room the night before His crucifixion when Jesus sat down with His closest friends to break bread and give thanks. Jesus said something that echoes through eternity: "Do this in remembrance of me" (Luke 22:19). That was the beginning of what we celebrate as the Last Supper—the foundation of Communion. But Jesus was also inviting us into something more than just the ritual. He was reminding us that meals can be life-giving when we come together around the table and invite Him to join us.

There's also the beautiful parallel to the daily bread that Jesus taught us to pray for in the Lord's Prayer, because back then a daily meal wasn't guaranteed. People had to rely on God's provision. Ironically, in today's world bread gets a bad rap. Carbs! Gluten! Just ask my doctor (he's very aware of my relationship with Chicago deep-dish pizza). My wife's latest obsession is making sourdough bread from this 1970 starter she got. It is delicious . . . and, apparently, it is healthy? Sourdough starter is a whole production, though: You have to feed it, babysit it when you're out of town, keep it alive. It's basically like a pet you can make sandwiches with! The point is that whenever we invite people over for dinner now, she bakes bread from that same starter. So, spiritually speaking, I wonder whether we should just go in for seconds on the bread. When we break bread together and pause to pray, we're doing what Jesus did—remembering who gave us the bread in the first place.

I know we live in a fast-food, DoorDash, eat-on-the-go culture. But I wonder what would happen if we slowed down a little and turned mealtime into sacred space again? One of my favorite moments at our family gatherings is when my dad, the West family pastor, leads us in a prayer before we eat. It's not rushed; it is reverent. It recenters us on who is most important. In a world moving at lightning speed, sometimes that pause to pray and share a meal is exactly what we need in order to remember who we are and how good God is. I want to challenge you not to underestimate the power of sharing a meal and a prayer. Be intentional to create the space to pause, invite God in, and pray for your daily bread. And don't forget the name cards, because you never know who needs to be reminded: You belong here.

PRAYER CHALLENGE

This week, make it a goal to sit down and share at least one intentional meal with family, friends, or neighbors. Before the meal, pause and pray—not just for the food but for the people around the table. Thank God for the gift of shared moments and daily bread. If you're feeling bold, write name cards for your guests (even if it's just on paper scraps) to remind them they're wanted and welcomed.

PRAYER JOURNAL

1. When was the last time you paused and gave thanks before a meal? What shifted in your heart when you did?
2. Who in your life might need a seat at your table right now? How can you extend the love of Jesus through hospitality?
3. What does breaking bread with others mean to you spiritually (not just socially)? How does it remind you of Jesus' presence?
4. How might your family life, friendships, or faith deepen if you made mealtime prayer a consistent habit?

chapter 26

PRAY IN SOLITUDE

Learning the power of solitude was not a lesson I chose but one I learned the hard way. I've written about the season of my life when I was forced to have vocal cord surgery and went through several weeks when I couldn't speak at all. I couldn't talk with my wife, I couldn't joke with my kids, I couldn't sing a note. While all the uncertainty of that situation made it one of the most challenging times of my life, it was also the quietest. And it proved to be a catalyst for huge spiritual growth. Because I couldn't communicate, I retreated to my music studio and spent hours by myself, unsure of what to do with all the words trapped inside me.

In the middle of that season, a friend gave me a book by Henri Nouwen called *The Way of the Heart*. It is a book that has had a dramatic impact on my faith. It explains the role of silence in the life of a believer and the power of praying in solitude. It changed everything for me as I began to understand just how uncomfortable I was with being alone in the quiet. I would have much rather had the noise of a baseball game in the background, a podcast playing in my earbuds, or music filling up the silence. But sitting by myself with no distractions? That was painful until I began to understand that God wanted that space in my life.

Nouwen explained how we enter solitude not to be lonely but to meet Jesus, to be with Him and Him alone. I learned that only in a place of solitude can we bring our wounds to Jesus and allow Him to heal us. The reality is that when we get intentional about solitude, something holy happens. In that quiet space we can confront the truth of who God is and, just as important, who we are to Him. In the years since that experience, I've come to terms with how important it is to be intentional about having some prayer time in solitude. It's so much easier to stay busy, keep my emotions numbed by noise, surround myself with people at all times, and avoid thinking too much about my flaws and failures. But purposefully finding time to be alone with God is transformative. Those times of solitude invite us to sit at the feet of Jesus and accept the eternal truth that we are loved just as we are—it is like recharging your spiritual batteries.

Only in a place of solitude can we bring our wounds to Jesus and allow Him to heal us.

We see an example in the story of Jacob in the Old Testament that sheds a little different light on solitude with God. The night before he was going to face his estranged brother, Esau, Jacob sent his family and all his possessions away, and the Bible tells us he was "left alone" (Gen. 32:24). In that place of solitude, Jacob was met not with comfort but with a wrestling match! He wrestled with a mysterious figure through the night, refusing to let go until he received a blessing. That quiet, isolated moment turned out to be the turning point in his life. Yes, Jacob walked away with a limp, but he also emerged with a new name. Alone and stripped of every distraction, Jacob finally came face-to-face with God, and it changed him forever. His story reminds us that solitude isn't always serene. Sometimes you'll find that God wants to wrestle with you about the realities of your life that don't align with His will. But it's in those times of discomfort that deep transformation can begin. Like Jacob, we may not emerge from solitude untouched, but we will come out blessed, changed, and more fully who God created us to be.

When I first began embracing solitude in my prayer practice, it felt foreign and awkward at times. I didn't always hear dramatic revelations. Sometimes it felt as though nothing was happening at all. But over time I began to notice a change. I began to embrace the reality that, in the stillness and the quiet, I felt less alone, because God was drawing near. And that solitude is simply the very holy work of coming before the heavenly Father with our full attention. Maybe you're scared of what you'll hear or afraid of what you won't if you sit in the solitude before God. Maybe you're addicted to distraction because the stillness feels too risky. But I want to encourage you that the place of quiet prayer is where He reminds you that you are His beloved child. Solitude in prayer is where healing begins, where rest is found, and where peace comes to fullness.

PRAYER CHALLENGE

This week, carve out ten minutes each day to sit in complete silence with God with no phone, no music, no distractions. Maybe you can begin by simply praying, "Here I am, Lord." Don't rush and don't worry about what you should hear or feel. Just be present and let Him show up.

PRAYER JOURNAL

1. How comfortable are you with solitude in your prayer life right now?
2. What distractions most often keep you from sitting still and being fully present before God?
3. When you imagine being alone and fully present with God, what emotions arise?
4. How might your relationship with Jesus grow if you made solitude a regular part of your prayer life?

chapter 27

PRAYER AS A COMPASS

These days, if you set out on a road trip without GPS, you're either incredibly brave or just stubborn. With Waze, Google Maps, and the other apps that can reroute you around traffic jams or road construction, there's no shortage of assistance in finding the best route to wherever you want to go. Yet somehow, even in a world full of digital maps and turn-by-turn directions, we still manage to get lost when it comes to navigating life. If getting lost were a sport, the Israelites in the Old Testament would have made it into the hall of fame. God delivered them from slavery in Egypt with miracle after miracle—a parted sea, a pillar of fire, plagues of locusts and frogs, all kinds of shock-and-awe stuff. But, after all of that, they still tried to make their own way without Him and ended up wandering the wilderness for forty years. And it's easy to shake our heads at them until we realize how often we do the exact same thing. God offers us wisdom and guidance, yet so often we insist, "No thanks, I'm good," only to find ourselves wandering in circles and wondering where we went wrong. I've had my share of "wandering in the wilderness" moments too!

Not too long ago I decided to try out a new trail at Percy Warner Park in Nashville. It was a hot and humid Tennessee summer day, and I thought a quick hike would be the perfect way to get outside. I picked the new red trail, completely unaware that it was one of the longest and hardest routes in the park. Somewhere along the way I got a little turned around. Despite the clearly marked paths, I couldn't figure out how to get back to my car. The heat was brutal, my water bottle was empty, and I started to panic a little. The worst part of the whole thing? I was less than two miles from my house. I passed a few people on the trail—twice, actually—but I was too embarrassed to stop and ask for help. I was confident that I could figure it out on my own. I was so wrong.

Eventually, after several hours of wandering, I found a picnic table, sat down in the shade, called my wife, and prayed that she could find me. After a lot of driving and searching the various lots around the park, she finally did. I was sweaty, dehydrated, and feeling a little ridiculous. "No one can ever know about this," I said with a laugh as she drove me home. It's a funny story now, but at the time it revealed something real about my heart. I learned that pride is often my default setting. I would rather struggle on my own than admit I need some help or direction. It reminded me of how often we trust our own instincts and move ahead without asking God for directions only to find ourselves lost, confused, and exhausted. How many times have we taken the long way around simply because we didn't pause to pray and ask God for direction?

I am learning that God intends prayer to be our first instinct rather than our last resort. I don't want to wait until I'm lost in the wilderness to consult my compass. I want to consult the compass from the start! I want efficiency. I want direct answers. I want to know exactly where I'm headed and how fast I'll get there. But God doesn't always work that way.

Sometimes He leads us down winding paths. Sometimes He invites us to trust Him in the wandering. And sometimes, when we refuse to ask for directions, He lets us wander until we realize how much we need Him. And, occasionally, He will even treat us as He did Saul in the Bible, before he became Paul, who, on his way to Damascus, was struck by a blinding light from heaven. Then "he fell to the ground and heard a voice" (Acts 9:4). Yes, at times God whispers to get our attention, and He can also knock us flat on our backsides when we need it. Saul needed that brick-through-the-window moment to turn him in the right direction. Honestly, sometimes we do too!

The beauty is that no matter how lost we get, no matter how long we've been wandering, God always meets us when we finally stop to pray and ask for His help. He is never too far away to guide us back. If you feel like you're lost right now—if life feels confusing, overwhelming, or just too much—maybe it's time to stop trying to figure it out on your own. Maybe it's time to pray, not as a last resort, but as your first step in finding the right direction. God is not playing hide-and-seek with your life—in fact, I think He prefers that we ask for help before we get lost. I promise you that the heavenly Father is ready to lead you and guide you. He's ready to be your compass—if you're willing to stop, pray, and listen.

PRAYER CHALLENGE

This week, before making any major decision, pause and pray first. Ask God for His direction and resist the urge to rely solely on your instincts. Pay close attention to any places where you sense His leading, even if it's not the direction you expected.

PRAYER JOURNAL

1. What keeps you from asking God for direction consistently—pride, fear, busyness, or something else?
2. Think about a current decision you are facing. How can you intentionally invite God into that process through prayer?
3. How would your life change if prayer became your compass instead of your backup plan?

chapter 28

PRAY "IN JESUS' NAME"

When my daughter started kindergarten, I remember sitting around the dinner table eager to hear all about her first big day of school. She was absolutely beaming as she shared the news, "I made a new best friend today!" Naturally, my wife and I wanted to know more. "What's your best friend's name?" we asked her. She paused, scrunching her nose and thinking hard for a moment, before finally shrugging and saying, "I don't know. But she's my best friend!" We laughed about that for a long time, but even years later I find myself thinking about that story and how it pertains to my spiritual life sometimes.

There have been so many moments in my life when I have lived out that very story in the same way. Why? Because I have a best friend in Jesus. Just like the line from that old hymn says—what a friend I have in Jesus! And I know He is my Savior, my closest companion, and my Redeemer. But in the busyness of life, I sometimes forget to pause and remember the earth-shaking, stone-rolling, resurrection power that His name holds. I too often forget that when it comes to my prayers, the name of Jesus isn't just a "Christianese" way to sign off. The name of the Savior isn't a religious formality—it is the very foundation and authority on which we pray!

The Bible tells us that when we pray in the name of Jesus, we are standing on the fullness of who He is. In the gospel of John, Jesus promised His followers, "And I will do whatever you ask in my name, so that the Father may be glorified in the Son. You may ask me for anything in my name, and I will do it" (14:13–14). And then, in John 16:23–24, Jesus explained, "Very truly I tell you, my Father will give you whatever you ask in my name. Until now you have not asked for anything in my name. Ask and you will receive, and your joy will be complete." The emphasis couldn't be clearer: *in His name.* We are not praying based on our own merit, our own strength, or our own goodness. We are praying based on the eternal, unshakable authority of the Son of God. In fact, every name given to Jesus throughout Scripture reminds us of just how much power we are calling on when we pray:

Jesus is the Wonderful Counselor.
He is Jehovah-jireh, the God who provides.
He is Emmanuel, God with us.
He is the Prince of Peace.
He is the resurrection and the life.

So when we pray in Jesus' name, we are calling on every part of who He is, and that means every promise, every victory,

I HAVE A

best friend

IN JESUS.

and every truth. The apostle Paul wrote in Philippians, "At the name of Jesus every knee should bow, in heaven and on earth and under the earth, and every tongue acknowledge that Jesus Christ is Lord" (2:10–11). Paul said it: at the name of Jesus! Not at the name of a social media influencer, the president of the United States, a bestselling author, or even a beloved mentor—only at Jesus' name will every knee bow. At Jesus' name every tongue will confess. At Jesus' name every power will submit. When I pray, I am not asking in my name or by my authority. I am praying under the banner of the resurrected King, the One who conquered death, crushed sin, and holds the keys to eternity.

One of my favorite moments in worship is when we sing songs that proclaim the beauty and the power of His name!

> What a beautiful Name it is . . .
> What a wonderful Name it is . . .
> What a powerful Name it is
> The Name of Jesus Christ, my King[1]

The Bible makes it clear that truth isn't just poetic—it's full of power. His name is the foundation that gives our prayers their strength.

Maybe today you feel as though your prayers have lost their power. Maybe you've been praying for something for a long time, and discouragement has started to creep in. Maybe you've begun to wonder whether your prayers make any difference at all. If that's you, I want to encourage you to come back to the Name. Remember in Whose authority you pray! Our prayers are never insignificant when we offer them to the Name above all names. When you pray in Jesus' name, you are declaring that you trust not in yourself but in the One who has already won the victory. So let's remember that a prayer in Jesus' name is a prayer that holds more power than we could ever imagine!

PRAYER CHALLENGE

This week, as you pray, intentionally slow down when you speak the name of Jesus. Reflect on the attributes of who He is as your Friend, your Savior, your Healer, your Provider, your Peace. Let the reality of His name shape your prayers, filling them with boldness and trust.

PRAYER JOURNAL

1. How often do you pause to consider the meaning and power behind the name of Jesus when you pray?
2. Which attribute or title of Jesus brings you the most comfort right now? Why?
3. When you think about the authority you have in prayer because of Jesus' name, how does that change your confidence when you approach God?
4. What specific prayer request in your life needs to be surrendered fully under the power and authority of Jesus' name this week?

chapter 29

PRAYERS OF REPENTANCE

I grew up singing in my dad's church. And to this day I still love the old hymns we used to sing. One of my favorites has that powerful line "What can wash away my sin? Nothing but the blood of Jesus." I still remember that chorus ringing out through the sanctuary as the congregation sang. When I sing those words, I believe them. But when it comes time to live them out, especially through honest prayers of repentance, that's where it gets harder. Most of us would rather avoid that uncomfortable space where we admit we've messed up. Even in everyday relationships it's hard to admit, "I was wrong." Instead, we choose to say things like "I'm sorry *you* felt that way" or "I'm sorry if *you* misunderstood me," sidestepping the real issue, which is . . . us! Unfortunately, that instinct to deflect runs even deeper when we're talking to God.

King David knew that feeling quite well. After committing numerous sins with Bathsheba, such as adultery, deception, and even murder, having orchestrated her husband's death, David finally broke down. When the prophet Nathan confronted him, David didn't deflect or make excuses. He simply and honestly confessed, "I have sinned against the Lord." And in the aftermath of that moment, David wrote one of the most honest prayers of repentance we have in Scripture: "Create in me a pure heart, O God, and renew a steadfast spirit within me" (Ps. 51:10). He knew he couldn't undo what he had done. But he also understood something even more powerful: God was merciful. David didn't try to hide—he brought his sin into the light so that healing could begin. I think that's what honest repentance looks like.

Our confession is not the moment He finds out about our sin; it's the moment we stop pretending.

Sometimes we think of confession as breaking bad news to God, but it's really just confessing what He already knows. Our confession is not the moment He finds out about our sin; it's the moment we stop pretending. That's where true freedom begins. I'll never forget a letter I once received from a woman who had carried a secret for more than thirty years. In her words, it was a wound she had never spoken out loud, not even to her husband of thirty years. She told me about the guilt she had carried after an abortion, something she had buried deep for so long. When I asked her why she would set her secret free in a letter to me of all people, she confided, "Honestly? I never thought you'd read the letter. It just felt good to set that secret free." What she didn't realize is that it wasn't about me at all. In writing those words, she was finally bringing her pain and her shame to Jesus. And the truth? He already knew. He wasn't surprised. He had already paid for it. She went on to confide in her husband, who wholeheartedly forgave her. It healed some real brokenness in her life. She began to discover true freedom and now volunteers at a crisis pregnancy center, willingly sharing the story she once worked so hard to hide.

I know we often imagine repentance before an angry judge in some kind of courtroom scene, but the Bible paints a way different picture. Repentance isn't about condemnation but about walking into the light, where shame loses its grip. Confession isn't about groveling before an angry king—it's about turning to a heavenly Father whose mercy runs way deeper than our worst mistakes. When we hide our sin and shame, we actually forfeit the freedom Jesus died to give us. Think about that! We carry the guilt that He already carried to the cross. But repentance isn't about being crushed by regret; it's about receiving the grace that sets us free. As the apostle Paul wrote in Romans, "Therefore, there is now no condemnation for those who are in Christ Jesus" (8:1).

> **Don't stop praying honest prayers of repentance, because they're the very prayers God will use to set you free!**

There is *no* condemnation. No fear of being exposed or rejected. Only grace and freedom. What does that really mean? It means no sin is so dark that it requires a second sacrifice, because when Jesus declared "It is finished" from the cross, He meant it. One sacrifice and one Savior. One name that washes every stain completely clean. So when we offer prayers of repentance, we're not trying to earn forgiveness. We're finally receiving the forgiveness that has already been given. We're not approaching a throne of judgment; we're sitting down at a table where a chair has already been pulled out for us. Maybe today you're carrying something you've tried for years to hide. Maybe you've convinced yourself it's too late, too heavy, or too shameful to bring to God. I promise you it's not. Bring it into the light, confess it, surrender it to Jesus. Don't stop praying honest prayers of repentance, because they're the very prayers God will use to set you free!

PRAYER CHALLENGE

Take time this week to pray an honest prayer of repentance. Pray about whatever you have been carrying, without editing, without making excuses—just bring it before Jesus. Thank Him that His forgiveness covers you completely and ask Him to help you walk forward in freedom.

PRAYER JOURNAL

1. What emotions do you notice when you think about praying a prayer of repentance?
2. Is there a hidden burden you have been carrying that God is inviting you to surrender today?
3. How would fully embracing God's forgiveness change the way you live out your faith?

chapter **30**

PRAY FOR PEACE

I've always loved the scene in the New Testament when the disciples wake up Jesus on that boat in the middle of a raging storm. The gospel of Matthew includes my favorite version:

> Suddenly a furious storm came up on the lake, so that the waves swept over the boat. But Jesus was sleeping. The disciples went and woke him, saying, "Lord, save us! We're going to drown!" He replied, "You of little faith, why are you so afraid?" Then he got up and rebuked the winds and the waves, and it was completely calm. (8:24–26)

The first reaction from the guys closest to Jesus, who had seen the miracles firsthand, wasn't to be calm, cool, and composed. They became panicked and desperate over the roar of the wind and crashing waves.

Remember, these were grown and capable men, some of them very experienced fishermen, and they were freaking out and convinced they were about to die. Somewhere in the back of the boat while this was going down, you know what Jesus was doing? He was fast asleep. It's a lot easier to relate to the disciples' reaction when the waters of life get a little choppier than we want to admit. When storms crash into our lives, when anxiety, fear, and uncertainty threaten to capsize our fragile boats, we often choose panic over prayer. It's a good thing that Jesus doesn't get frustrated by our freak-outs. He simply stands up, speaks peace over the chaos, and reminds us that the size of the storm never threatens His power. And I think He uses these moments to challenge us to let go of fear and embrace faith just as He did with His disciples.

I know what it feels like to carry around anxiety and worry. I've had times when I've felt like I was in a storm—my mind wouldn't stop racing, robbing me of peace. Worry has a way of hijacking our thoughts and convincing us that peace is impossible. Every time I hear the Christmas-carol line "Sleep in heavenly peace," I realize how rare that kind of peace actually feels in the hurry and noise of everyday life. Sleep, peace, and rest seem like unattainable luxuries when life's storms blow through. It seems like all the rage these days are the podcasts, books, and YouTube videos about the importance of managing stress and getting sleep to live longer and healthier lives. But maybe what we really need isn't another how-to podcast or another peace-promising supplement. Maybe what we need is found in prayer—the kind of prayer that helps us surrender what we were never meant to carry to the One who can calm any storm.

Throughout the New Testament, Jesus offered His peace. Not just a small measure of peace, but a deep, abiding peace that surpasses all understanding. In the gospel of John, as He was preparing His disciples for His departure, He told them, "Peace I leave with you; my peace I give you" (14:27). He also said, "I have told you these things, so that in me you may have peace" (16:33). It's a peace He offers freely, even when the storm is still raging around us. The apostle Paul wrote, "And the peace of God, which transcends all understanding, will guard your hearts and your minds in Christ Jesus" (Phil. 4:7). He made it clear that this kind of peace doesn't come from *understanding* our circumstances. And it doesn't depend on whether the storm stops or the outcome changes. Paul was talking about the deep and abiding supernatural peace that Jesus offers.

I think there is another really important lesson in this. We cannot share the peace of Jesus in our lives if His peace isn't first residing in our hearts. When we fail to seek His peace, it shows up in all kinds of ways. We become anxious leaders who micromanage everything and everyone around us. We become impatient parents who snap at the people we love most. We become too anxious or afraid to make a difference in the world. If we don't intentionally pursue peace in prayer, we will be ruled by the anxiety, worry, and panic that threaten to sink the boat every time a storm comes.

We cannot share the peace of Jesus in our lives if His peace isn't first residing in our hearts.

I want to challenge you that when Jesus offers us His peace, it's not just for our own sake. It's so we can become peacemakers and peace carriers to an anxiety-ridden, storm-filled world. But when we let His peace take root in our hearts through prayer, He empowers us to live differently. We can be living examples of a different way of being in the world to our families, to our neighbors, and to the people sitting next to us on the subway or walking past us at the grocery store.

Receiving God's peace transforms us, and when His peace lives in us, we can step into His calling to become peacemakers. If you find yourself feeling tossed by the waves, or restless with worry, remember the truth that Jesus is still the One who calms the wind and the waves. He's still the Prince of Peace, and His invitation to you remains the same: "Come to me, all you who are weary and burdened, and I will give you rest" (Matt. 11:28).

PRAYER CHALLENGE

This week, every time you feel anxiety rising or your thoughts spiraling, stop and pray this simple prayer: "Jesus, bring Your peace into this moment." Take a deep breath and surrender whatever you are carrying to Him.

PRAYER JOURNAL

1. When was the last time you felt overwhelmed by the storms of life? Did you respond with panic or prayer?
2. What situation in your life right now feels like it is stealing your peace? What would it look like for you to surrender that situation to Jesus in prayer today?
3. How might your relationships change if you consistently chose peace over panic in your everyday life?

chapter 31

PRAY FOR HEALING

I believe that whenever we say a prayer for healing, we're stepping into a vulnerable place where we admit that something is broken, and no matter how strong or smart or determined we are, we can't fix it ourselves. There's this moment of healing in the Gospels that gets me every time. A father brought his suffering son to Jesus, and his prayer was beautifully honest: "I do believe; help me overcome my unbelief!" (Mark 9:24). And what did Jesus do? He didn't shame him for his doubts. He didn't say, "Come back when your faith is a little stronger." Instead, Jesus responded with compassion. He healed the boy. Because our Savior doesn't hold back His perfect love just because we have imperfect faith. He's looking for open, willing hearts to bring whatever faith they've got, even if it's just a mustard seed's worth.

Emotional.
Spiritual.
Eternal.

Throughout the Gospels, Jesus is known as the Great Physician. Blind eyes were opened. Lepers were made clean. The lame were told to get up and walk. A woman who had been bleeding for twelve years was restored. The miracles go on and on, and most of them involved healing. But we live in a world where healing doesn't always happen the way we hope. I've prayed for kids in the pediatric cancer ward, for friends in the ICU, and for people facing impossible diagnoses. Sometimes healing comes, and sometimes it doesn't. And I can't ever pretend to understand why . . . not fully, not on this side of eternity. But I do know that God is always doing a deeper work when we pray for healing.

When we look closely at Jesus' miracles, physical healing was never actually the finish line. It was often the doorway to something more important to Him: hearts mended, spirits restored, relationships with God repaired. In Mark 2, when a paralyzed man was lowered through the ceiling by his friends, Jesus didn't start by fixing his legs. He probably astonished the onlookers when He started by working on his soul: "Son, your sins are forgiven" (v. 5). Only then did He attend to the physical ailments. "Get up, take your mat and go home" (v. 11). Healing with Jesus is never just skin-deep; it's emotional, spiritual, eternal.

He restores our souls, He rewrites our stories, He redeems our sins, and He's still doing it today.

I haven't faced the kind of desperation in praying for healing that many of my friends have experienced. But I've had a brush with physical brokenness. There's a scar on my left forearm—it's faded over the years but still jagged from the hundred-something stitches it took to close the wound. It is a reminder of the time when I was about to sign my first major record deal. I had big dreams, big plans, and I believed they all hinged on my showing up with a guitar in hand. Then came the injury. I couldn't hold a guitar pick. Couldn't grip a pen. Couldn't tie my shoes. I prayed hard for healing, thinking I was just praying for my arm, but God had much more in mind. In that slow, painful recovery, He wasn't just repairing nerves and tendons, He was healing something deeper. He was pulling the pride out of me, rewriting my dreams, and shifting my heart from performance to purpose. I had been telling God how I wanted Him to use me, and as I prayed for healing, He showed me that He could use me even if I never played another chord. That kind of healing doesn't show up on an MRI, but it's for real and it lasts.

Maybe you're carrying the kind of wounds today that don't show up on any scan. Wounds from betrayal, divorce, loss, or abuse. Maybe the hurt came from someone who claimed to speak for God. Maybe you trusted someone deeply and ended up hurting quietly. I want you to hear that those invisible wounds are real, and they matter to God just as much as any physical ailment. He wants you to bring those injuries to Him in prayer.

Jesus doesn't need your prayer for healing to be polished. And it doesn't have to be full of certainty. Because when we pray for healing, we're not just asking God to fix what's broken. We're surrendering ourselves and admitting we can't do any of this on our own. And that kind of honest prayer for healing is powerful. The good news is that our helplessness doesn't mean

OUR SAVIOR DOESN'T HOLD BACK HIS *perfect* LOVE JUST BECAUSE WE HAVE *imperfect* FAITH.

hopelessness. When you know who holds your story, you can bring your broken pieces to Him without fear. Because our God, the Great Physician, doesn't just heal our bodies—He restores our souls, He rewrites our stories, He redeems our sins, and He's still doing it today.

PRAYER CHALLENGE

This week, take whatever broken piece you have been carrying, whether physical, emotional, or spiritual, and bring it honestly to God in prayer. Don't hide your doubts or minimize your pain. Try trusting Him with your hurt and your hope.

PRAYER JOURNAL

1. What area of your life feels like it needs healing right now, physically, emotionally, or spiritually?
2. When you think about your past wounds, how have you seen God use them to do a deeper work in your heart?
3. How does remembering Jesus' compassion for the doubting father in Mark 9 encourage you to pray even when your faith feels small?
4. What would it look like for you to stop trying to fix things yourself and instead completely surrender your need for healing to God?

chapter 32

PRAY EVEN WHEN YOU DON'T FEEL LIKE IT

There are many days in my life when I find it easy to pray. You know the kinds of days when gratitude pours out naturally, when you feel God's nearness, when prayer seems more like breathing than working. And then there are days when you wonder whether you can bow your head even one more time. The days when your faith feels dry as a desert, when your heart feels tired, when it seems as though heaven is silent. What should you do on those days when praying seems more like pushing the world uphill than anything? I am learning that you bow your head anyway, and, no matter how many times you've already prayed, you do it one more time.

In my journey as a songwriter, I've learned something important about the discipline of sitting down and writing in those "I don't feel like it" moments. There have been so many days when I've sat at the piano or picked up my old Gibson and felt convinced that I had nothing left to say. There are plenty of days when writing another song feels impossible and inspiration seems a million miles away. The funny thing is that those are the very moments when I am on the precipice of something. Because every time I hit that wall and I decide to fight through, every time I decide to show up anyway, something beautiful eventually breaks through. Many of my favorite songs were written on the days when I least felt like writing. And you know what? The same has been true in my prayer life.

We've covered so many important aspects of prayer throughout this book, but it occurred to me that maybe you need to hear today the same truth that I need sometimes: You're not a bad Christian if you don't always feel like praying. Look, the reality is that while our feelings are real, they are not a reliable compass for faithfulness or God's presence. We spend a lot of time in our culture talking about how we feel. It's a popular way to start a conversation: "I feel . . ." The truth is, though, that our feelings aren't always connected to reality. And our feelings about God aren't always connected to how much He loves us and is faithfully walking with us every step of our day. A mentor of mine told me that praying when you don't "feel" God's closeness is part of strengthening your faith. I am learning that choosing to pray when you don't feel like it might just be one of the most powerful acts of worship you ever offer.

You're not a bad Christian if you don't always feel like praying.

PRAY

anyway.

The Bible gives us plenty of examples of this kind of faithfulness. One of my favorites is Elijah in 1 Kings 18. Elijah had just witnessed an incredible victory, complete with fire falling from heaven and the defeat of 450 prophets of Baal. God's power was on display for all to see. Elijah was coming off the kind of spiritual high that would carry us for months. But what happened next? Elijah ran away and hid. He was scared for his life. In fact, he told God he was done.

He said, "I have had enough, LORD" (1 Kings 19:4). In a moment when we would expect Elijah to be on fire with faith, he was exhausted and discouraged. But even in his despair, Elijah kept talking to God. And God met him where he was, not with judgment, but with provision.

He sent an angel to feed Elijah and gave him rest. God arrived not in fire and earthquakes but in a gentle whisper to remind Elijah that he was not alone. When I read Elijah's story, I'm reminded that those "I'm giving up" moments can be the most powerful times of prayer.

So wherever you are today, whether you feel strong and spiritually energized or tired and disconnected from God, I challenge you to pray anyway. Bow your head anyway. Open the Bible and pray the Psalms. Get on your knees (or sit in the quiet of your car for a moment) and open your heart to God in prayer. I promise you that God honors a faithful heart that shows up even when it doesn't feel like it. That is what a maturing faith looks like. Remember—the depth and meaning of your prayers are never really connected to your feelings. Let's keep choosing faithfulness over our feelings, because prayer is reaching out to a faithful God who *always* feels like hearing from you.

PRAYER CHALLENGE

This week, commit to five minutes of prayer each day, especially on the days when you feel distracted, busy, or uninspired. Bring whatever you have, even if it's messy or you're tired. Trust that God will meet you there, just as He met Elijah in the wilderness.

PRAYER JOURNAL

1. When was a time you prayed even though you didn't feel like it? What happened afterward?
2. How does Elijah's story encourage you in seasons of emotional or spiritual exhaustion?
3. What are some practical ways you can remind yourself to stay faithful in prayer when your emotions don't feel strong?
4. How might regular prayer, even when it's difficult, renew your passion and connection with God over time?

chapter **33**

PRAYERS OF MOURNING

There is a line from Psalm 30 that shows up in memes everywhere: "Weeping may last for a night, but joy comes in the morning." Those words sound poetic and hopeful, but the reality is that when you're experiencing a dark night of the soul, the morning can often feel a long way off. The idea of joy returning someday can sound like a distant dream. Yet the enduring promise of the Bible is that God draws close to those who are hurting. Psalm 34:18 says, "The LORD is close to the brokenhearted; he rescues those whose spirits are crushed" (NLT). That verse doesn't say that grief will be quick or that sorrow will be simple, but it does promise us God's presence. When we pray in our grief and sorrow, God meets us in that sacred space.

I think it is important to remind ourselves that grief isn't evidence of weak faith or a sign that we've given up hope. If anything, our mourning is further evidence that this world is broken. I think about the moments after a funeral when the crowd has gone home and the friends who brought over casseroles have moved on with their lives. Those times when the sympathy cards have stopped coming, the phone isn't ringing, and we are left alone with our grief. It is in the silence of mourning that God really shows up. Even when no one else understands the shape or size of the ache you carry, He knows.

When we pray in our grief and sorrow, God meets us in that sacred space.

I always take heart in knowing that Jesus understood grief and loss. When Mary and Martha sent word that Lazarus had died, Jesus didn't arrive right away. When He finally did, He saw Mary's tears, and even though He knew that He was moments away from calling His dear friend Lazarus back from the grave, He still wept. The gospel of John tells us plainly, "Jesus wept. Then the Jews said, 'See how he loved him!'" (11:35–36). That moment has always moved me. Jesus, the Son of God, who had power over death itself, grieved so deeply that even onlookers recognized how much He loved Lazarus. The tears He shared with Mary at the loss of His friend point to the holiness of grief as an expression of love.

I've had conversations with people who've experienced tremendous loss, and they all echo the same truth—grief doesn't follow a timeline. It doesn't politely end after six months and go away. A friend of mine lost his little sister twenty-five years ago, and even now he still can find himself hit by fresh waves of grief at the most unexpected times. That doesn't make him weak. It

GRIEF DOESN'T FOLLOW A *timeline.*

makes him human. Grief can come in many forms when we lose something we care deeply about: a job, a relationship, our health, or even our dreams. Usually, our instinct is to try to rush through these experiences, numb them, gloss over them, or ignore them altogether. But God never asks us to fake our way through grief. He simply invites us to bring it to Him in prayer and in honesty and allow Him to sit with us in those experiences.

What if we practiced praying through our grief, not just when it's fresh and raw, but over the long haul? What if we made space to sit with God in the heaviness and allowed Him to carry what we no longer could? What if we allowed our tears to become prayers? Psalm 147:3 reminds us, "He heals the brokenhearted and bandages their wounds" (NLT). I love how the apostle Paul described God as the Father of compassion and the source of all comfort in 2 Corinthians 1:3–4: "Praise be to the God and Father of our Lord Jesus Christ, the Father of compassion and the God of all comfort, who comforts us in all our troubles." But he didn't stop there. Paul explained that God comforts us in our troubles *so that we can learn to comfort others*: "So that we can comfort those in any trouble with the comfort we ourselves receive from God." What a beautiful redemption of grief and mourning—that our pain can lead to someone else's healing, that our comforted hearts can become a safe place for someone else to grieve. When we pray through our grief, as painful as it is, it can become the soil where compassion grows. It can deepen our trust, strengthen our faith, and connect us with others who will walk the same road.

Whenever we sit with God in our grief and mourning and bring those feelings to Him in tears or in whatever words we can muster, we also have to take hold of Jesus' promise from the Sermon on the Mount: "Blessed are those who mourn, for they will be comforted" (Matt. 5:4). Jesus didn't say, "They might be comforted." He didn't say, "Someday, maybe it'll happen." It is a statement made with the bold certainty of resurrection truth that we can cling to for our times of mourning and offer to others: "They *will* be comforted."

PRAYER CHALLENGE

This week, if you're grieving something or someone, take a few moments each day to sit quietly in God's presence. You don't need to say much. Just invite Him in. If you know someone who is grieving, ask God to show you how to be present for them too.

PRAYER JOURNAL

1. What kind of loss are you carrying right now—something recent or something from long ago?
2. How has God already shown up in your grief, even if only in small ways? What would it look like to invite Him into the quiet moments when grief hits hardest?
3. Who in your life is grieving that you could simply sit with, as Jesus did with Mary and Martha?

chapter 34

PRAY FOR THE PRODIGAL

At my concerts these days, I carry a prayer wall with me to every city. It's a pretty simple setup somewhere out in the lobby with some tags, pens, and a place where people can write down prayer requests and hang them up. But I've noticed that it has become one of the most meaningful parts of what we do on tour. At the end of the night, after the music fades and the lights come down a little, my team brings that prayer wall onto the stage. And as I stand there reading through those handwritten prayers, it changes the way I see every face that fills that room. Behind every ticket, every seat, every smile there is a story, a victory, a battle, or a heartbreak.

Almost every night, without fail, I find several prayers hanging on that wall that say "I'm praying for my prodigal to come home." Sometimes the handwriting is messy, sometimes it's even tearstained, but there is a longing behind those notes—a mom, dad, grandparent, or friend who is heartbroken and desperate, clinging to hope for that one lost soul. Those prayers always stop me in my tracks. I think about the tears that must have been shed before those words were written. I think about the sleepless nights and the whispered prayers. And I am inspired by the faithful hearts who haven't given up, who keep on hoping even when the waiting feels unbearable.

When I wrote the song "Don't Stop Praying," part of the inspiration came from situations just like these, for my family and for the people like us who are praying difficult prayers for the lost loved ones that haven't yet been answered. That's why the line "Don't stop praying for the prodigal" found its way into my song. Because the hardest prayers are the ones we feel like we've been praying forever with nothing to show for them. So why do we keep praying for the prodigals? Why do we keep praying for the lost souls who seem to have wandered too far from home and too far from God's love? Because of the good news.

We can show up and keep praying because of how the story of the prodigal son ends. In Luke 15, Jesus told the story about a young man who rejected his family and wasted everything he had. He ran from home, spent his inheritance on wild living, and eventually found himself broke, hungry, and desperate. Finally, with no place else to go, he decided to come home. He came not with demands but with a broken heart, ready to ask his father for mercy and forgiveness. And here's the part that gets me every time, the moment when the prodigal's father first saw his lost son: "But while he was still a long way off, his father saw him and was filled with compassion for him; he ran to his son, threw his arms around him and kissed him" (v. 20). The father wasn't sitting on the porch with his arms crossed ready to give his son a lecture, nor was he hanging back suspiciously waiting for an apology. The father didn't shame him; he ran to him, hugged him, and threw a huge party for him.

Now, it was interesting to learn that in the culture of that time a man of stature never ran anywhere. It would've been considered humiliating to run. In fact, running was something only children or servants did, not the patriarch of a household. But this father didn't care about appearances. His complete joy overwhelmed any sense of pride. It brings me to tears when I think about the truth that Jesus is teaching us about the love of the heavenly Father in this parable. The father in Jesus' story ran to the prodigal because that's how God's love runs to us. That's the kind of grace God has for His lost children. And the hope of that love fuels our prayers for the prodigals in our lives.

So when you pray for your lost son, your wandering daughter, your struggling friend, or your unbelieving parent, your prayers are aligned with the heart of God. You are agreeing with the truth that our Savior leaves the ninety-nine to go after the one who is lost (Luke 15:4–7). And a prayer in agreement with God's love is powerful. I don't know who comes to mind when you read this today. Maybe it's someone who has walked away from their faith or someone who has never known the love of Jesus.

Maybe your prodigal is a person whose choices have led them so far off course that finding their way back seems impossible. I hope you'll take heart as you whisper one more prayer and know that the Father is standing on the horizon watching for them. And when God sees that familiar face appear in the distance, He won't just wait. He's going to run with His arms outstretched.

The Bible tells us that day is coming, and, until it does, don't stop praying. And when that homecoming moment finally happens, whether on this side of heaven or the next, there will be a celebration unlike anything we have ever known.

PRAYER CHALLENGE

This week, choose one prodigal or lost soul you know and commit to praying for that person every single day. Write his or her name on a note where you will see it often—on your bathroom mirror, dashboard, or phone lock screen. Each time you notice it, pray a simple, hope-filled prayer: "God, run after them. Bring them home." Trust that heaven hears every prayer and that God never stops pursuing.

PRAYER JOURNAL

1. Who is one person in your life right now you are praying will come home to God?
2. How does the story of the prodigal in the Gospels give you hope in your waiting?
3. What emotions do you experience as you pray for someone who is wandering? How do you bring those emotions to God?
4. How can you encourage others who are also waiting and praying for their prodigals?

chapter 35

PRAY FOR RENEWAL

The world may say having a "childlike faith" is naive, but I disagree. Children are wide-eyed, eager, and full of imagination about what God can do, and they lack the burden of cynicism that adults often carry. There are qualities of childlike faith that we should eagerly embrace. Remember that when Jesus' followers asked Him who was greatest in the kingdom of heaven, He didn't point to the most accomplished faith leaders or the most seasoned preachers. Nope. He pointed to a child and said, "Unless you change and become like little children, you will never enter the kingdom of heaven" (Matt. 18:3). That line has stuck with me over the years, especially when I start feeling as though my prayer life is getting a little . . . well . . . old. Now, I don't mean old in the sense of wise; I mean when my faith becomes a little tired, routine, and disconnected from the wonder that my heavenly Father is always present and listening to me.

I've been a Christian for more than three decades, and if I'm being honest, there have been many seasons in my life when I've replaced passion with passivity. When I've gone through the motions of faith but lacked the fire. When I've traded a spiritual hunger for religious routines. And it's not that I have ever stopped believing in God. But at times in my life, I've stopped approaching Him with the curiosity and awe of a child. That's why I believe that asking God for renewal in our hearts (and in our faith) can be the most important prayer we can pray.

There is a great moment in the gospel of John when Nicodemus, a respected religious leader, met with Jesus under the cover of night to ask Him about how to enter the kingdom of God. Now, Nicodemus wasn't seeking religion; he already had plenty of that and was after something much more meaningful. And Jesus told him the truth: "You should not be surprised at my saying, 'You must be born again'" (3:7). Jesus explained that he must be born of the Spirit, have a fresh start, a renewed faith, a heart reborn. The apostle Paul said that this type of renewal isn't a onetime event but a way of life for the follower of Jesus: "Therefore we do not lose heart. Though outwardly we are wasting away, yet inwardly we are being renewed day by day" (2 Cor. 4:16).

> Asking God for renewal in our hearts (and in our faith) can be the most important prayers we can pray.

Sometimes we get confused thinking spiritual renewal happens only at a revival service. The truth is that God can bring

WHERE DO YOU NEED THAT *renewal* RIGHT NOW?

renewal in the pedestrian and simple moments of quiet prayer. I'll never forget one normal Sunday service when God met me in the middle of an old hymn. Nothing dramatic happened externally, but something quietly reignited in me. My passion for ministry had grown weary. But in that moment God gently turned my attention back to Him, and I felt renewed, not just as a minister or an artist, but as a child of God. That moment showed me that renewal doesn't always arrive in thunder and lightning and lead-guitar solos and big emotions. God can awaken the wonder of a child in your heart right now in the most everyday, ordinary prayer time. We need that renewal now more than ever.

Paul's words in Romans 12:2 have never felt more relevant than they do in the world we're living in today: "Do not conform to the pattern of this world, but be transformed by the renewing of your mind." God uses prayer to renew our perspective, reshape our priorities, revive our passion, and give us that childlike wonder about what He can do in our lives. One of my favorite quotes from a book called *Fresh Wind, Fresh Fire* says it this way: "The more we pray, the more we sense our need to pray. And the more we sense a need to pray, the more we *want* to pray."[1] That's the essence of a prayer for renewal. It's not driven by guilt or fear but fueled by a hunger to know Jesus more and bring more Jesus to the hurting world that needs Him.

God can awaken the wonder of a child in your heart right now in the most everyday, ordinary prayer time.

We're living in a time when revival is showing up in unexpected places—on college campuses, in coffee shops, in quiet corners of everyday life. And the heartbeat of every revival is always prayer. Not flashy or polished—just real, raw prayer from people like you and me who are tired of living spiritually disconnected. I want to remind you today that we are only one prayer away from another revival that can begin with renewal in your heart. So let me ask you: Where do you need that renewal right now? Is there a relationship that feels distant? A purpose that feels forgotten? A spiritual fire that's flickering low? Is it your marriage? Your mindset? Maybe it's your priorities? Maybe, like me, you've let your faith settle into autopilot and get a little old. Wherever you are today, I believe God is ready to restore that passion and childlike wonder to your faith. All you have to do is ask.

PRAYER CHALLENGE

This week, set aside one day to unplug from your normal routine and intentionally spend time asking God for renewal. Think about the areas where your faith feels tired or where your joy has dimmed. Ask God to renew your mind, restore your heart, and reignite your passion for Him. Close your time by reading Romans 12:2 aloud and praying it as a promise.

PRAYER JOURNAL

1. Where in your life do you feel as though your passion for God has faded into routine?
2. What does "childlike faith" mean to you right now, and how could you begin to return to that posture in prayer?
3. What's one small, intentional step you can take this week to invite spiritual renewal into your daily life?

chapter 36

PRAY LONG-DISTANCE PRAYERS

I've heard it said before that if you ever feel a distance between you and God, He's never the one who moved. I've had plenty of moments in my life when I felt as though God was a long way away from me. I think we all go through those times. I've known what it's like to feel spiritually distant, distracted, as if the sound of my voice in prayer might not make it through to God. But here's the good news of the Bible: There's no such thing as long distance in God's kingdom. There is never a signal loss, there are never dropped calls, and heaven doesn't have spiritual time zones. The reality of the gospel is that there is never any distance too great for God to come close to you. And no matter how life can make you feel, there is never a prayer too far away to be heard.

I've spent a lot of time on the road in my career. Usually that means that my tour bus rolls out of Nashville more than seventy nights a year and carries me across the country from one zip code to another. And while I'm grateful for technologies of connection such as FaceTime, phone calls, and text messages, none of it is ever the same as being home. It's a pathetic substitute compared to sitting at the kitchen table with my girls hearing about their days firsthand. When I am away, there's still a distance I feel and a longing to be close that no technology can satisfy. Isn't it incredible to know that with God it's so much different? We can't outrun His presence, and we can't ever be too far away from His grace. No matter how many millions of miles and time zones you cross, you can never escape His love. One of the clearest messages of Scripture is that God specializes in closing the distance between you and Him. The whole message of the entire Bible is that when we wandered away, God came closer. When we built walls, He tore them down. When sin separated us from Him, He sent Jesus to carry a cross up a hill and build an eternal bridge that couldn't be broken.

We talked about the story of the prodigal son, which is really the story of us all. We've all put distance between ourselves and the Father who loves us. But remember—that story ends with a Father who runs toward us. He is always covering the distance to meet us, even in our long-distance prayers. And if you need a beautiful example of long-distance prayer in action, look no further than the Roman centurion in Matthew 8. He came to Jesus, not for himself, but on behalf of his sick servant who was miles away. "'Lord,' he said, 'my servant lies at home paralyzed, suffering terribly.' Jesus said to him, 'Shall I come and heal him?' The centurion replied, 'Lord, I do not deserve to have you come under my roof. But just say the word, and my servant will be healed'" (vv. 6–8). He believed that Jesus didn't need to travel

THERE IS
NEVER A PRAYER
TOO *far* AWAY
TO BE HEARD.

to heal his servant. He trusted that the power of God wasn't limited by proximity or location. And Jesus was amazed by his faith. In fact, Jesus said He hadn't seen faith like that anywhere in Israel! And what happened next? The servant was healed from a distance.

Maybe you need to be reminded that God doesn't need a GPS to find you today. He doesn't need you to cover any distance, because the power of prayer isn't about your location. It's about His abiding presence. The words of the apostle Paul remind us: "For I am convinced that neither death nor life, neither angels nor demons, neither the present nor the future, nor any powers . . . will be able to separate us from the love of God that is in Christ Jesus our Lord" (Rom. 8:38–39).

Nothing can separate us! Not our mess-ups. Not our silence. Not even the million miles of our mistakes. That road you think is too long to come back from—He's already erased it. That spiritual distance you feel—He is still only a whisper away. So, if today you feel far away from God or if your prayers feel like they have to travel light-years just to reach His ears, I want you to remember that He is the God running toward you, the One who heals from any distance, the One who is right now as close as your next breath and your next prayer. Next time you feel like you are millions of miles away, I want you to take a deep breath, offer up a prayer, and allow God to show you how He has been right there next to you every step of the way.

PRAYER CHALLENGE

This week, every time you're tempted to feel as though God is far away, lean in to that feeling by whispering a simple prayer. Think about one area in your life where you've felt distant from God and ask Him to meet you there. He will. Remember—what you think is a long-distance prayer is heard instantly by your loving heavenly Father.

PRAYER JOURNAL

1. Have you ever gone through a season when God felt distant? What did you learn during that time?
2. What "distance" do you believe disqualifies you from praying right now—busyness, guilt, apathy?
3. How does the story of the centurion's faith encourage you when you pray for someone who feels far from God?
4. If nothing can separate you from God's love, what's stopping you from coming back to Him in prayer today?

chapter **37**

PRAY FOR YOUR FAMILY

I'll never forget walking past my parents' bedroom as a kid and hearing my mom and dad whisper prayers for me. At the time I didn't understand the power in what they were doing, and I didn't give it much thought. But now, as an adult, I realize how much those committed prayers have affected my life. Each day, they were doing battle, lifting up the family before the Lord. They prayed for me and my brothers, our aunts and uncles, and our grandparents and cousins—for all of us. I know Dad has prayed over us at dinners, church services, road trips, and family celebrations for years, but I have never been able to shake the realization that he and Mom had a liturgy of praying for us each day.

I can tell you these days nothing brings me to my knees more consistently than praying for my own family. And for more than just the obvious dad moments, like watching my daughter turn out of the driveway in her car and praying she gets somewhere safely. No, there are random moments, even right in the middle of a workday, when I feel an urgency to stop and pray for my wife and my girls. This compulsion to pray for my family reminds me of a verse from Acts that always jumps out at me: "They all joined together constantly in prayer, along with the women and Mary the mother of Jesus, and with his brothers" (1:14). There's something so moving about how even Jesus' own family was part of that prayer gathering. Scripture says "constantly" in prayer. Jesus' family, who had walked and talked with Him, lived and ate with Him, saw the importance of praying for one another "constantly" as they waited for what God would do next.

It's funny how much time we spend thinking about how we are going to provide for our families. I'll stress over sticking to budgets and saving for college and making sure everyone has what they need. And those are good things. But the reality is that the most important legacy I can leave my kids isn't financial—it's spiritual. I think about my parents' daily prayers, and I know that I want my house to be a house of prayer. I want my kids to know that, long before I tried to help them with their problems, I was praying for them.

And since we are talking about praying for our families, we need to be reminded that praying is the opposite of worrying. Yes, it's a natural inclination to worry about our loved ones' health, their futures, and their faith—but what if that is just a prompting to pray? The apostle Paul has offered us a better framework in Philippians 4: "Do not be anxious about anything, but in every situation, by prayer and petition, with thanksgiving, present your requests to God." And then he added something beautiful: "And the peace of God, which transcends all understanding, will guard your hearts and your minds in Christ Jesus" (vv. 6–7). That's the kind of peace I want in my home. And the only way we get there is through prayer. Not through performance or perfect parenting, but persistent, faithful prayer.

Maybe prayer wasn't part of your upbringing. Or maybe you come from a family where faith wasn't a thing. Here's an amazing truth with Jesus: You can start something brand-new—you can be generation number one in your family. Maybe you can start a legacy of prayer that reaches future sons and daughters and grandchildren you haven't even met yet! Proverbs says, "Train up a child in the way he should go; even when he is old he will not depart from it" (22:6 ESV). What if your commitment to prayer is the seed that sets that promise in motion for generations to come?

What if your commitment to prayer is the seed that sets that promise in motion for generations to come?

I've seen firsthand what happens when someone refuses to give up praying for her family. My grandmother prayed for years and years that my grandfather would quit drinking and start going to church. She didn't see the change right away. But she never stopped praying. And eventually he gave his life to Jesus in a small, humble church in Mason City, Iowa. Not long after, he started showing up every Sunday with my grandmother and their ten kids. My dad jokes that the size of the congregation doubled the first Sunday the West family attended! That one answered prayer changed the trajectory of our family forever.

People talk about family trees, but I think we need to start focusing more on *spiritual* family trees. Maybe we can ask some tough questions of our family: What kinds of roots are we putting down in our prayer life? Are we showing up each day to sow seeds of prayer into our family story? Because when we do that, we're inviting God to build a legacy that can have an impact on the world. So let's embrace the practice of praying constantly over our families, as the early church family did. Let's pray boldly, as my grandma did. As my parents do. Let's release the worry and, with every prayer, bring new life to our family tree.

PRAYER CHALLENGE

Choose three family members to pray for by name every day this week. Ask God to guide, protect, and draw them closer to Him. If you feel led, send one a simple message: "I prayed for you today." You might be the first person who ever has. Let this be the week you start a legacy of prayer in your family.

PRAYER JOURNAL

1. Who in your family weighs most heavily on your heart right now? Write down their name and ask God to meet them where they are.
2. What would it look like to make your home more of a house of prayer? What's one simple step you can take this week?
3. What kind of spiritual roots are growing in your family tree and what kind do you want to leave behind?

chapter 38

PRAY HOLY SPIRIT PRAYERS

I know the topic of praying in the Holy Spirit might make a few readers shift uncomfortably in their seats. Depending on your church background, it might bring up memories of times that felt a little outside your comfort zone. Maybe somebody in your life "put the *ghost* in Holy Ghost" for you, if you know what I mean. As a kid I was at a church camp where I felt the discomfort of being pressured to pray in tongues. In that moment it didn't feel like a God thing for me; it felt like a performance. So I get the uneasiness some people have about it. But, as we explore praying in the Holy Spirit, I'm not focusing on speaking in tongues (although Scripture does include that in Acts as one of the Spirit's gifts). What I do want to talk about is something important that can help grow and mature your prayer life: inviting the Holy Spirit to guide you when you pray.

The apostle Paul explained the importance of this in Ephesians 6:18: "And pray in the Spirit on all occasions with all kinds of prayers and requests. With this in mind, be alert and always keep on praying for all the Lord's people." That's not uncomfortable—it's powerful. To "pray in the Spirit" is to be fully present in your prayer, to open yourself to God's presence and power, and to let the Spirit lead your thoughts and words.

In the Gospels, Jesus described the Holy Spirit as our Advocate, the One who would teach and remind us of the truth. He told the disciples, "All this I have spoken while still with you. But the Advocate, the Holy Spirit, whom the Father will send in my name, will teach you all things and will remind you of everything I have said to you" (John 14:25–26). That means when we come to prayer, we are not on our own. We don't have to try to figure out the right words by ourselves. The Holy Spirit is interceding, reminding, and guiding. Paul painted an incredible picture of this: "In the same way, the Spirit helps us in our weakness. We do not know what we ought to pray for, but the Spirit himself intercedes for us through wordless groans . . . because the Spirit intercedes for God's people in accordance with the will of God" (Rom. 8:26–27). That blows me away every time. When we run out of words, when we're too sad, too tired, too confused, the Spirit steps in and speaks for us.

Praying in the Spirit is allowing God to realign our desires. It's about surrender and trust. I'll never forget a moment when I experienced this kind of prayer firsthand. I was in Estes Park, Colorado, at a Christian music conference I hadn't even planned to attend. Some folks, whom I didn't know, said they felt led by the Holy Spirit to pay my way there. I was a broke college student and couldn't have gone otherwise. But I just trusted and

INVITE THE

Holy Spirit

TO GUIDE YOU WHEN

YOU PRAY.

went, and I ended up leading worship in front of artists and producers. That unexpected excursion led to my getting signed to my first open doors in the music industry. But, more than that, it was the Spirit gently nudging me toward something I didn't even see coming. I guess you could say it was a holy "yes" that started with a Spirit-prompted prayer.

Holy Spirit prayer doesn't just happen in special places or situations such as church services or devotional hours. It happens in the car, in hospital waiting rooms, on early-morning runs, while folding laundry or doing dishes. And when you invite the Holy Spirit into your prayer time, He will show up! Sometimes in a whisper, like "Call that person" or "Stop and pray right now." At other times it can feel like getting hit over the head with a two-by-four of truth—as with my experience of being prompted to turn my car around and go beg my way out of a country-music deal that would've led me away from music ministry. No matter how the Spirit shows up, He is always drawing you back to the Father. Maybe you remember the lines from that old worship song that say, "Holy Spirit, You are welcome here." Well, that's the posture of empowered prayer. When we invite the Holy Spirit into our prayers, we start participating in God's story and intention for us. The Spirit helps us listen, respond, and grow. So I want to challenge you today, no matter your background, to start inviting the Spirit to guide you in prayer. Allow Him to pray when you can't, shape your words when you don't know what to say, and align your desires with the heart of your heavenly Father.

PRAYER CHALLENGE

Each day this week, begin your prayer with this simple invitation: "Holy Spirit, You are welcome here." Then pause, listen, and allow Him to lead your words or your silence. He already knows what you need.

PRAYER JOURNAL

1. Are there ways your view of the Holy Spirit has been shaped more by people than by Scripture? How can you recenter that view?
2. What does it mean to you to "pray in the Spirit"? How could your prayer life grow in that direction?
3. What would change in your daily life if you made space to say, "Holy Spirit, You are welcome here"?
4. Have you ever felt the Holy Spirit prompt you to pray or act? What did you do in response?

chapter 39

LAST PAGE OF THE BIBLE PRAYERS

I've always loved the idea that our prayers are *never* without hope when we consider them through the lens of eternity. If you know my story, you know that one day after middle school when I was trying to watch a Cubs game on TV, I found Jesus while watching a Billy Graham sermon I accidentally stumbled across. I am really fond of Billy Graham, and I've always found this one quote from him particularly inspiring: "I've read the last page of the Bible. I know it's going to come out all right."[1]

Graham preached around the world for six decades, to an estimated 215 million people, and he served as a spiritual adviser to US presidents, so I've always been encouraged that, with all of his experiences in the world, he could say that confidently. I think deep down we all want that kind of reassurance when we pray. We all want to know that no matter how painful, uncertain, or confusing life gets, the story ends in restoration. Those words inspired one of my favorite songs I've written, called "The Last Page of the Bible," where the chorus encourages: "Trouble may last for a moment / And weeping may last for a night / But I've read the last page of the Bible / And it's all gonna be all right."

That's the deepest hope we hold on to as Christians. We can pray expectant prayers in the valley, prayers for reunion in our grief, and courageous prayers in our brokenness, because as followers of Jesus we already know that the last chapter of the story has been written, and the tomb is empty! What an empowering promise that every longing we lift up in prayer, whether for healing, justice, peace, or redemption, will find its ultimate answer in eternity. I believe we're given one of the most comforting visions in all of Scripture in Revelation 21:4: "'He will wipe every tear from their eyes. There will be no more death' or mourning or crying or pain, for the old order of things has passed away." This isn't just poetic language, it's a concrete promise from God about what He has in store for us. The old order, marked by suffering and sin, will be replaced by a new reality. And that's why we keep praying. Because even when we don't see the answer right away, we trust that everything broken now will one day be made whole.

The apostle Paul took this even further when he wrote that "the creation itself will be liberated from its bondage to decay and brought into the freedom and glory of the children of God" (Rom. 8:21). Paul's words remind us that it's not just people who are waiting for redemption—the *entire world* is groaning for it. Our prayers join in with the longing of creation itself, which is

WHENEVER WE
PRAY WITH THE
LAST PAGES OF THE
BIBLE IN OUR HEARTS,
OUR PRAYERS GET
bigger, bolder,
AND *braver.*

calling out for renewal. That's the scale of what we're participating in when we pray!

And, in Philippians 3:20–21, he continued, "But our citizenship is in heaven. And we eagerly await a Savior from there, the Lord Jesus Christ, who . . . will transform our lowly bodies so that they will be like his glorious body." That means this life isn't our final address. We're not just hoping for a better day; we're expecting that our Savior will finish what He started. Even our physical bodies, subject to weakness and decay, will be renewed to match the glory of Christ. So when we pray with that kind of future in view, we can boldly declare the promises of God over our lives.

I think whenever we pray with the last pages of the Bible in our hearts, our prayers get bigger, bolder, and braver. We stop whispering in fear and uncertainty and start declaring in faith. When we pray from the confidence of knowing God is setting everything right, we can face the impossible as people who understand the love of their heavenly Father.

Jesus tells us in Revelation 22:12, "Look, I am coming soon! My reward is with me, and I will give to each person according to what they have done." This is one of the last promises in all of Scripture, reminding us not just that Jesus is returning but that He is coming back *with purpose*. That means the prayers we pray, the acts of love we offer, the battles we fight each day—none of it is wasted. So here's what I've been asking myself more often, and I'll ask you too: Do you pray like you *know* how your story ends? And do you live life like you know that the outcome is already decided? What would it look like for us to allow this enduring biblical truth to reshape our prayer lives moving forward? What if we allow it to influence every prayer, knowing that, in the end, every need will be met, every cry heard, and every heartache made whole? I say we start to pray each day like the people who've read the last page—and trust God's promise that it's all gonna be all right.

PRAYER CHALLENGE

This week, pray with the end in mind. Each day, take one burden, something that feels uncertain or broken, and speak God's eternal promise over it. Let your prayers be shaped by the confidence that the last page has already been written, and it ends in healing, redemption, and joy.

PRAYER JOURNAL

1. How does knowing the last page of the Bible influence your view of unanswered or delayed prayers?
2. What would change about your prayer life if you believed that Jesus is coming again and that every wrong will be made right?
3. How can you shift your focus toward eternity in the way you pray and live each day?

chapter **40**

DON'T *EVER* STOP PRAYING

We've reached the final pages of this devotional, and I hope that through these forty days you have found a new anticipation for what God is doing, a fresh sense of purpose in your faith, a revived and refreshed understanding of the power of prayer. And while this may be the last few pages, I hope you will see it as the beginning of your prayer journey. Over the previous chapters, we've explored what it means to follow the Father's voice, to pray in the valleys, to lift others in prayer, and to pray with courage and commitment. But now comes the part where it moves from the page to your life. This is where you decide that prayer isn't just something you read about—it's something you live out in your daily life, in your family, and in your faith community.

Let's revisit my story at the beginning of the book about that father-daughter retreat and how my daughter had to walk blindfolded through the woods and listen to *only* my voice. I'll never forget the moment she called out, "Dad, are you there?" And how everything changed when, after waiting and watching, I could finally speak into her journey. Of course, that story wasn't just about Lulu or our relationship; God used it as a great lesson for me to learn the power of prayer. It reminded me that He is always watching over me. I hope it was a good reminder for you, too, because we all drift away at times and forget to pray. It is such an important lesson to remember that every time we call out, He's right there!

Also, let me say this as clearly as I can: Don't just say you're going to pray for someone or about something—actually pray. Don't talk about it—pray right here, right now, in the moment. I find that if I tell someone I'll pray for them, I can forget and get sidetracked, so I just do it right there when they ask! I'll never forget a moment backstage during a meet and greet. A woman and her husband approached me and told me she had been diagnosed with cancer and was scheduled for surgery the next morning. Usually, with a line of people waiting, I would've said, "I'll be praying for you." But this time I said, "Let's pray right now." And we did. We prayed right there in the middle of the noise and the crowd. A year later that same husband and wife came through the line again at another show and told me how God had brought healing to her life. It reminded me that prayer is earnest and urgent! Just like Psalm 28:2 says: "Hear my cry for mercy as I call to you for help, as I lift up my hands toward your Most Holy Place." Our prayer is a cry for help, a lifting of hands, a reaching toward heaven in

> Every time we call out, He's right there!

Prayer ISN'T JUST SOMETHING YOU READ ABOUT—IT'S SOMETHING YOU *live out* IN YOUR DAILY LIFE, IN YOUR FAMILY, AND IN YOUR FAITH COMMUNITY.

faith. David taught us that we can go to God boldly, honestly, and often. That's what prayer warriors do, and that is what I want to learn to be.

At the Apple Blossom Festival in Virginia recently, we set up a prayer wall right in the middle of the celebration. People wrote down everything from health needs to broken relationships to shattered dreams. Some of the prayer tags just had a single name written on them. But each one of them held the same truth that everyone is fighting a battle. I always take a moment to tell the crowd that there's not a single request written and stuck to the prayer wall that caught God by surprise. He hears every word, He knows every situation, and He is one prayer away. I love the example in Acts 12 when Peter was put in prison but the church earnestly prayed for him. That night, an angel of the Lord appeared, and Peter's chains fell off while the guards slept. He walked out of the prison, miraculously freed, and went to the house where many were gathered in prayer. When he knocked, they were astonished to see their prayer had already been answered. That's the power of a prayer!

I am hopeful that this book is just the beginning. God never leaves us right where we are in our faith but is always leading us to grow closer to Him. That means there is still a lot for you and me to learn about prayer. We always have room to grow and discover how and when to pray. My prayer, as you read these words, is that this book, which began with the truth that our heavenly Father is always just one breath away, will be the catalyst for Him to mold and shape you into a prayer warrior. Because what our world desperately needs are Jesus followers who understand the unfathomable and eternal power of prayer. As you go into your day, may prayer become your reflex, your rhythm, and your lifeline, and may it shape your thoughts, direct your steps, and be the fuel for your relationships. I hope you will join me in embracing the very foundation of being a disciple of Jesus, and don't stop praying—not now, not ever. Amen.

PRAYER CHALLENGE

This week, start a habit of in-the-moment prayer. When someone shares a need, stop to pray out loud right then and there. Write names on your mirror or calendar. Set reminders on your phone. Start praying as if your life—and theirs—depends on it. Because it does.

PRAYER JOURNAL

1. What keeps you from praying in the moment? How can you begin to break that habit today?
2. Who in your life needs you to become a committed prayer warrior for them right now?
3. What does Psalm 28:2 remind you about how we can approach God?
4. What next steps do you feel God is challenging you to take in your prayer journey?

NOTES

CHAPTER 6

1. C. S. Lewis, *Letters to Malcom, Chiefly on Prayer* (Harcourt Brace, 1963; repr., HarperOne, 2017), 111.

CHAPTER 28

1. Ben Fielding and Brooke Ligertwood, "What a Beautiful Name," Hillsong Lyrics, accessed July 17, 2025, https://hillsong.com/lyrics/what-a-beautiful-name.

CHAPTER 35

1. Jim Cymbala, *Fresh Wind, Fresh Fire: What Happens When God's Spirit Invades the Heart of His People* (Zondervan, 1997), 50.

CHAPTER 39

1. Billy Graham, "Billy Graham's Message for the Hopeless," sermon, originally titled "Hopeless, Yet There Is Hope," recorded in 1975 in Albuquerque, New Mexico, posted June 27, 2020, Billy Graham Evangelistic Association, YouTube video, 26:54, https://youtu.be/8sU2eShsojY?si=UScGRz0rGIVOZxEQ.

ABOUT THE AUTHOR

MATTHEW WEST has built his career as a revered storyteller. The five-time GRAMMY nominee, dubbed by Billboard as "one of Christian music's most prolific singer-songwriters," has been awarded multiple RIAA Gold & Platinum certifications, notched 30 number one songs combined as an artist and songwriter, and has more than 250 songwriting credits to his name. Matthew is passionate about providing hope and healing through the power of prayer and story. Matthew and his wife, Emily, live in Nashville with their two daughters, Lulu and Delaney.

ABOUT THE WRITER

MATT LITTON is a collaborative writer with three *Publishers Weekly* and *Wall Street Journal* number one bestselling books. He is passionate about partnering with talented artists, pastors, and thought leaders to craft stories and books that inspire change and make a lasting impact in the world. His recent projects include *Come Home for Christmas* by Matthew West (with Matt Litton), *On Our Knees* by Phil Wickham (with Matt Litton), and the devotional *In the Presence of Jesus* by Matt Litton and Paul Bane. You can explore more of Matt's work at mattlitton.com or follow his latest adventures on Instagram @MattLittonWriting.